Luiz Guilherme Dias Cesar

People Management and organizational culture change

Luiz Guilherme Dias Cesar

People Management and organizational culture change

Contributions and strategies for programmed processes of cultural change

ScienciaScripts

Imprint

Any brand names and product names mentioned in this book are subject to trademark, brand or patent protection and are trademarks or registered trademarks of their respective holders. The use of brand names, product names, common names, trade names, product descriptions etc. even without a particular marking in this work is in no way to be construed to mean that such names may be regarded as unrestricted in respect of trademark and brand protection legislation and could thus be used by anyone.

Cover image: www.ingimage.com

This book is a translation from the original published under ISBN 978-613-9-67063-5.

Publisher:
Sciencia Scripts
is a trademark of
Dodo Books Indian Ocean Ltd. and OmniScriptum S.R.L publishing group

120 High Road, East Finchley, London, N2 9ED, United Kingdom
Str. Armeneasca 28/1, office 1, Chisinau MD-2012, Republic of Moldova, Europe
Printed at: see last page
ISBN: 978-620-8-10815-1

Summary

ACKNOWLEDGMENTS

I'd like to thank all my family, without whom I certainly wouldn't be writing this document.

To my parents, Luiz Paulo Cesar and Lùcia Helena Dias Cesar, and my sister, Beatriz Dias Cesar, who fought so hard for me to have this chance. I understand how much it took for this to happen and I'm very grateful for everything.

To my aunt Luciléia Dias Moreira, for all the support she gave me and my family during the most difficult times. I will never forget her and I hope to be able to return one day. Special thanks also go to my uncle Orlando Luiz Moreira and my cousins Débora Dias Moreira and Bàrbara Dias Moreira.

To my grandmother Ivone Martins Dias, my guide.

To my advisor, Victor Claudio Paradela. Thank you for your teachings and the opportunities for academic growth.

DEDICATORY

I dedicate this work to my grandfather Diomedes Jovem Dias, who has always supported me and to whom I owe everything.

SUMMARY

This paper discusses how the People Management (PM) area can contribute to the development of planned processes of cultural change in organizations. An analysis of the historical evolution of PM within organizations makes it clear that the area should not just be an objective-functional component within the organization. It is necessary to create a sense of belonging for people. The set of assumptions shared in an organization's culture serves a stabilizing function and provides meaning for the people who participate in it. Organizational culture is made effective through narratives. The anthropological concept addressed is that narratives are a mechanism for mobilizing people that has proved effective in the evolution of contemporary society. The narrative created collectively from the myths and symbols shared in people's collective imagination engenders the ability to cooperate around the same goal and in large numbers. Historically, culture has shown itself to be a call for change and not for the preservation of the *status quo*, as has become customary. This change in meaning has engendered the characteristics of postmodern society. As a result, traditional management theories are limited in explaining the turbulence that characterizes contemporary society. This moment has dissolved the organizational narratives that have been developed over the last few centuries. In addition, the emergence of a technological revolution, which brings with it the almost unrestricted automation of industries, increases the instability of society and organizations in general. As theoretical support, the framework adopted presents the contributions of various authors on the issues surrounding people management and the characteristics of changes in organizational culture. The concept of organizational culture and its importance for companies is analyzed, followed by a look at the main challenges to achieving cultural change and a review of the strategies that can help to promote this movement. The contributions made by management are also analyzed, based on an analysis of the historical evolution of the area within organizations and the anthropological justification for mobilizing people. The research came to the conclusion that People Management (PM) should not just be an objective-functional component within the organization. The strategic purpose of PM should be to manage organizational culture in order to create a sense of belonging for people.

Keywords: People management. Organizational culture. Planned organizational change.

1 INTRODUCTION

The current phase of globalization requires companies to constantly adapt in order to remain competitive and meet market demands. The volatile conditions of the world market illustrate the need for organizations to constantly adapt to the environment in which they operate. The world is going through a period in which the market has a very strong influence on the environment, making it necessary for organizations to constantly adapt and innovate in order to satisfy the latent needs of customers (SHIBA; GRAHAM; WALDEN, 1997).

The characteristics of today's market have never before been observed at other times in history. The abrupt speed, breadth and depth of the changes have had a systemic impact on organizations, the state and civil society (SCHWAB, 2016). This historical moment of systemic change is known as the Fourth Industrial Revolution, a time when the use of new technologies in the production of goods and services will be almost unrestricted. New technologies are merging the physical, digital and biological worlds in a way that creates great promise and possible dangers.

The emergence of a technological revolution that brings with it the almost unrestricted automation of industries is also a factor in changing the organization's relationship with the market (SCHAWB, 2016). This model is defined by the meeting of the unfolding of systems that were developed on the infrastructure of the previous digital revolution, representing a paradigm shift in labor market relations, the future of work itself and income inequality, with geopolitical and social consequences around the world (PERASO, 2016).

Thus, these demands require actions from companies that provide strategic positioning. Internal change through a cultural change project can be an effective mechanism that can bring a competitive edge to the organization, as well as providing the desired strategic positioning.

The topic is important due to the current volatile conditions of the world market, which require the organization to constantly adapt to the environment in which it operates. This topic is also relevant due to the analysis made of the role of People Management

(PM) in this process of adapting the organization to the new market model, bringing to light the importance of PM functions for the future of organizations. The current phase can also be examined by the predominance of knowledge and information, making people an extremely important resource for the success of any organization. As such, PM functions have become an essential component of organizational strategy, directly impacting on the social and economic success of any enterprise.

This work, which presents the results of the research carried out, is divided into four chapters, including this introduction. The next highlights the theoretical framework adopted, presenting the contributions of various authors on the issues surrounding the research problem. The first chapter analyzes the concept of organizational culture and its importance for companies; it then looks at the main challenges for bringing about cultural change and reviews the strategies that can help promote this movement. The second part of the theoretical framework looks at people management and its contributions, based on an analysis of the historical evolution of the area within organizations, the anthropological justification for mobilizing people and the strategic trends for the future of people management.

The next chapter is dedicated to presenting the research methodology. The research method used is presented, in accordance with the bibliography researched. The procedures for collecting and analyzing the data obtained are then demonstrated. And finally, the approach taken to processing the data.

Finally, the last chapter shows the case study used in the research. This part is structured around the presentation of the company, the description of the change process studied and the final considerations.

2 THEORETICAL FRAMEWORK

In order to reflect on the research problem addressed here, an analysis of the concept of culture is first proposed, bringing this definition into the context of organizations through organizational culture. The importance of this concept for companies and the contextualization of this variable are also observed. Under current conditions of constant change in the world, society and the market itself, organizational culture is even more important. This context demands incisive action from the organization in order to adapt it to the demands of the market. The text studies this adaptation through structured processes of change, analyzing the main challenges and the strategies that favor this movement.

The second section presents a review of the literature on the contribution of the People Management (PM) area. The first concept addressed is the anthropological view of the mobilization of *Homo Sapiens* in their history. The idea presented is that narratives based on myths, rites and symbols are a mechanism for mobilizing people that has proved effective in the evolution of contemporary society. Therefore, the correct use of narratives allows GP to mobilize people around a common purpose.

This section also proposes a historical review of the area of management in Brazil, listing the schools of administration, theories from abroad and the historical events that allowed these practices to develop in Brazilian companies. This review makes it possible to methodologically analyze the activities of management, with the aim of outlining the area's current strategic model. The review is also important for elucidating future trends. This means outlining some strategic trends for PM, i.e. stressing that the area should not just be an objective-functional component within the organization. It needs to be a kind of "guardian of the organizational culture", by creating a sense of belonging for people. In the practical field, the action of management engenders activities that add value to the business in the strategic sense of the area through internal consultancy, as well as outsourcing or eliminating activities that don't add value to the organization's business (for example, timekeeping, payroll, transport and related activities).

2.1) Organizational Culture

To begin defining culture, it is interesting to analyze the development of this concept historically. In this sense, Bauman (2011) states that this concept was developed and introduced in the third quarter of the 18th century. He also points out that, originally, studies on culture basically focused on the search to change the *status quo*, rather than preserving it, as later became common. For the author, the term culture is in itself a call to action. In the initial sense, this action referred to the change that the dominant classes of the time wanted to implant in the other classes, in other words, the vision of a new economic and political model. After the domination of this new model, "culture was transformed from a stimulant into a tranquilizer; from the arsenal of a modern revolution into a repository for the preservation of products" (BAUMAN, 2011, p. 15). This loss of original meaning would be the result of a long process of transformations in the modern world, bringing to light the notion of post-modernity. The framework of culture today is shaped around the individual, adjusting freedom to each person's responsibility for their choices (BAUMAN, 2011).

According to Giddens (2005), culture relates to the aspects that are learned by the members of a society, making cooperation and communication possible. These aspects form a common context for life in society. Culture therefore comprises both intangible aspects (beliefs, ideas and values) and tangible aspects (objects, symbols). The intangible variables form the content of culture, i.e. abstract ideas that provide meaning and direction to humans as they interact in the social world. The tangible variables make it possible to represent this content. The framework of tangible and intangible aspects engenders a society's culture, through norms and values that affect people's behavior.

Culture thus plays an important role in life in society by perpetuating the values and norms that drive people's behavior. This role is equally important today because it offers opportunities for creativity and change. Values and norms often change over time, evolving gradually and naturally. Of course, there is also the possibility of deliberately altering these two variables through a planned social construct of change

(GIDDENS, 2015).

Another important concept brought up by Giddens (2015) is that, even within a society, some values can be contradictory, thus giving rise to various codes of behavior. This idea of subculture - groups that reject society's values and norms - is interesting when analyzing how a culture changes. These groups can promote different values from those already accepted, inciting a change in the dominant culture.

In today's globalized world, it has become imperative for organizations to keep up with the recurring changes that are taking place in society and consequently in the market. Understanding these changes in the macro-environment and adapting the organizational culture in order to remain in the market is something that company management must take as essential. While the constant alteration of many variables affects the maintenance of the *status quo* or even the predictability of future scenarios, it also opens up various business opportunities for organizations.

It is worth highlighting the relationship between the culture of a country and the culture that manifests itself in organizations. When these concepts are applied to the analysis of an organization, the characterization of the organizational culture emerges. Cameron and Quinn (2006 *apud* GOBBI, 2012) point out that the prevailing culture in a certain region or country directly affects the organizations based there.

Hofstede's theory of cultural dimensions (1980 *apud* Santana *et al*, 2014) allows us to guide the organization's actions in relation to the national culture of the country where the organization is located. The five dimensions analyzed are: Distance to power, Individualism *versus* collectivism, Masculinity *versus* femininity, Adaptation to uncertainty and Long-term *versus* short-term orientation.

Power distance relates to the question of authority and hierarchy and how the group perceives and accepts the established order. It is defined as the extent to which members at lower hierarchical levels accept submitting to their superiors. It therefore defines the extent to which a group accepts the unequal distribution of power.

The question of individuality and collectivism refers to the intensity of the social bond between people in a given group. Individualism is linked to the preponderance of individual interests over collective interests, while collectivism is the opposite. This relationship strongly impacts the behavior of individuals and the behavior of the group as a whole.

As far as the analysis of masculinity and femininity is concerned, it's about the extent to which a given culture values attitudes linked to masculine or feminine stereotypes. In the first case, objectivity, strength and imposition tend to be cultivated. In the latter, relationships, understanding, affection and other "feminine" manifestations.

With regard to aversion to uncertainty, this is defined as the degree to which members of a group perceive themselves in situations that are uncertain or have never been experienced before. It reflects the feeling of discomfort and insecurity that such situations generate in people. Groups with a high degree of aversion to uncertainty tend to have a need for predictability, evidenced in a strong code of beliefs and behaviors.

Finally, the relationship between the predominant long-term and short-term orientation is evidenced in the expectation of a return in terms of reward and the results of tasks in terms of waiting time. In a group with a short-term orientation, there is a strong concern with establishing an "absolute truth" that can provide certainty and ready answers to the problems experienced. In groups with a long-term vision, individuals tend to believe that the truth depends on the context presented.

These aspects are valid for all countries, but the degree of intensity varies from one to another. Therefore, this analysis is useful for understanding the specific social factors of each national culture and thus adapting the organizational culture to these aspects in order to mitigate the possible conflict of interest.

According to Schein (2009), culture is an abstract concept that becomes objective and powerful according to the social and organizational situations derived from it. The author defines culture as a dynamic social phenomenon, which is experienced and recreated according to the interactions of its components and the behavior of the leadership, constituting a structure through rules and norms delimiting behavior. A group's culture, therefore, can be formally defined as: "a pattern of shared basic assumptions that has been learned by a group as it solves its problems of external adaptation and internal integration." (SCHEIN, 2009, p. 16)

In this sense, culture must be analyzed on several levels, from the most tangible to the most abstract manifestations. Schein (2009) divides this concept into three levels. The first is the level of Artifacts, the visible components of the group, such as the physical environment, clothing characteristics, myths and stories. Artifacts also include the organization's processes, as they delimit the behaviour and integrate the routines of the members. This first part is the superficial layer of culture, which is easy to observe but difficult to understand in depth without knowledge of the other levels. The second level is the Assumed Beliefs and Values, which define a position taken and validated by the group. Validation can be through a shared knowledge base that can be tested (such as economic issues) or a social validation of broader values that are difficult to test (ethics, for example). This level predates the group behavior observed at the first level. The last and third level is that of Basic Fundamental Assumptions, which refers to the set of concepts that the group believes to be a consensus for the constitution of its members' values and behavior. It is at this level where culture has its real power, "as a set of basic assumptions defines what we should pay attention to, what things mean, how to react emotionally to what happens and how to adopt in various types of situations." (SCHEIN, 2009, p. 29) Therefore, the pattern of basic assumptions that are shared and taken as truth will manifest itself at the level of artifacts and beliefs and values.

Schein (2009) also brings up an important concept regarding the relationship between organizational culture and the environment in which the company is inserted, emphasizing the importance of the environment for the constitution and maintenance of an effective model of this concept. Therefore, comparing the cultures of different companies by means of a best/worst ratio is unsustainable; the efficient organization is the one that manages to adapt to the environment.

Fleury (1987) points out that it is possible to distinguish between two ways of working with the concept of culture. The first model refers to the process of elaboration and construction of consensual knowledge about the meaning of the world. The second analysis refers to culture as an instrument of power and legitimization of the prevailing order. Fleury cites the study carried out by Linda Smircich, in which the author categorizes the knowledge developed about the term culture:

Smircich (1983) distinguishes between two main lines of research: the first focuses on culture as a variable, as something that the organization has; the second line of research focuses on culture as a variable, as something that the organization has.

conceives of culture as the root of the organization itself, something that the organization is. In the first line of studies, it is also possible to distinguish between those who define culture as an independent variable, external to the organization (the culture of the society in which the organization is inserted and which is brought in by its members) and those who define culture as an internal variable (organizations produce goods, services and cultural products such as legends, rites and symbols) (SMIRCICH, 1983 *apud*

Fleury, 1987, p.9).

Carrieri (2002) goes into more detail on how to approach the term culture in organizational studies. Starting from the concept of culture as a concrete object, it is possible to model and control it, as well as it being an image of the organization itself and the social reality in which it is inserted. The author also brings up another term that makes the analysis of organizational culture a little broader: "The culture of the organization can be apprehended as a single, consensual one, or as several, ambiguous and contradictory, the result of a historical process." (CARRIERI, 2002)

As will be elucidated in the course of the text, organizational culture in organizations is told and made effective through narratives. These are generally enunciated by the organization and can also be carried out by different internal groups. An organizational narrative that manages to align itself with the individual and/or collective narratives of the groups that belong to it tends to have more satisfactory results. The concept behind this study is that well-structured narratives are an efficient mechanism for guiding people, making them an extremely important tool for people management.

2.1.1 Importance for Organizations

The set of shared assumptions in an organization's culture serves a stabilizing and meaning-providing function for the people who participate in it. The evolution of culture is one of the means by which an organization preserves its integrity and provides itself with an identity of its own (SCHEIN, 2009). Therefore, organizational culture is important for the company in the sense that it gives people a sense of belonging to a certain group.

This role played by culture makes it possible to explain some of the less apparent aspects related to the behaviour of individuals within a group or organization. Once the set of shared assumptions is assumed to be true, it influences the behavior of the participants. Shared basic assumptions, based on common learning experiences, are a mechanism for understanding group behavior (SCHEIN, 2009).

According to Schein (2009), it is also possible to see that once this role played by culture has been established, several other critical elements are added to the analysis. The first refers to the structural stability it provides to a group, defining a certain type of behavior that is shared and stable. Changing behavior at this level is not a simple task. The second refers to the depth and intangibility of this concept when applied to a certain group. A behavior can be defined as one of the cultural manifestations, but not as the culture itself. The next element is the extent to which culture can affect the functioning of the group, i.e. how a group of people internalizes it and how it reflects in their behaviour. And finally, the standardization of the elements within a broader vision of the whole, implying rites, myths and symbols that are linked to a coherent whole.

Organizational culture can also be related to companies' financial performance. Although there is no definitive answer in the literature as to the degree of influence of this variable on financial parameters, some studies have already been carried out with the prerogative of evaluating the correlation between them. Cameron and Quinn (2006 *apud* GOBBI, 2012) refer to a study in which they identified the five US companies with the highest financial returns and compared them to companies in the same sector that did not achieve the same success. When analyzing the factors that led to success, the authors concluded that the differentiator between these companies was an intangible factor that was not clearly evident. The aspect of competitive differentiation that combined to the financial result was, in fact, the organizational culture that the company possessed.

Kotter and Hesket (1992 *apud* GOBBI, 2012) carried out a study of 207 different companies, relating the adaptability of their culture to their financial performance. The authors define an adaptable culture as one that encourages leadership at various levels and values employees, customers and shareholders. The results showed that companies that were able to adapt had higher financial indicators than those that didn't: growth in gross revenue (682% against 166%), growth in the number of employees (282% against 36%), share price appreciation (901% against 74%) and net revenue (756% against 1%).

The adaptability of a certain organizational culture is essential for the success of an organization, given the complexity of today's corporate environment. As the values practiced by society change, so do the norms that govern people's behavior. Points of view change, facilitating the emergence of new management models, which are influenced by the complex interaction between various social, technological and political factors. The structure of competing values in management is based on the assumption that the organization is faced with a complex and paradoxical world. It is necessary to adopt a set of diverse values that may seem contradictory, such as focusing on the future while remaining concerned with the present.

Based on an analysis of the four main management models described below, Quinn *et al* (2015) introduced the imperatives relating to each typology of culture, associated with the idea of the structure of competing values. The authors relate the historical moment in which each management model was developed to the dominant organizational culture in the company.

The first would be the Scientific Management model, using ideas from Taylor, Ford and others, which allowed the introduction of techniques to rationalize work. The authors call this model the "rational goal", in which the defined criteria for efficiency are productivity and profit. This approach brings the concept that clear direction translates into productive results. The imperative for action defined here is to compete. Subsequently, the second model developed is called internal process, related to the studies of Max Weber and Henri Fayol. This model complements the previous one, with stability and continuity as its criteria. The emphasis is on processes, based on the belief that the routinization of tasks leads to work stability. Here the imperative for action is to control (QUINN *et al*, 2015).

According to Quinn *et al* (2015), the human relations model was developed in the second quarter of the 20th century. From Elton Mayo's studies, which will be mentioned in the theoretical framework, we can see the need for a greater focus on the power of interpersonal relationships and informal processes in group performance. The main characteristic is that people's involvement results in commitment, with an orientation towards the development of cohesive teams. The imperative to collaborate is therefore adopted. From the 1950s onwards, technological advances began to occur more and more rapidly, thus changing society's values. Complementing the human relations theory, this open system model provokes the need to compete in an ambiguous and competitive environment. The criteria for organizational success are adaptability and external support. The imperative adopted here is to create.

The changes that took place in global capitalism during the 20th century engendered a constant movement related to change. According to Bauman (2013), the scenario of instability constitutes the transformation from modernity to the current format of the modern condition - post-modernity. The constant search for modernization, which characterizes the current era, is capable of pushing it to intensify itself, dissolving everything that is "solid" into "liquid". This movement is characteristic of the modern way of life, transforming society and its structures into something that cannot remain the same for long. Social organizations dissolve faster than it takes time to shape them, corresponding to a scenario of constant change.

None of the models already presented have been able to respond to the problems faced by organizations. Simplistic solutions, which usually define cause and effect clearly, have no longer been able to respond to the changes imposed by the environment. The attempt to create conditions to meet predetermined results, with a clear mapping of cause and effect, has become obsolete in today's conditions. The assumption of traditional theories of the constant search for balance through adaptation leads to a tendency towards only incremental changes, which occur gradually and predeterminedly. However, today's environment involves constant abrupt and profound changes.

It is from this set of factors that the theory of competing values was born. The integrative evaluation of this methodology makes it possible to integrate the four models proposed above. If the models are considered in isolation, they cannot provide effective answers for organizations. However, by analyzing each one as part of a larger structure, the options for action and potential effectiveness increase (QUINN *et al*, 2015). Because of its flexible and integrative form, the Competing Values framework presents a model for understanding organizational culture. Each of the management models presented tends to favour certain dominant characteristics in the culture of the organizations that adopt it.

Cla's culture, for example, is primarily concerned with the values and objectives shared by people, emphasizing the maintenance of the group. Effectiveness lies in the human capital and commitment of individuals based on the core values of trust, participation and a sense of belonging. Leaders of this type of culture tend to be facilitators of team interaction, trying to motivate the team towards cohesion, affiliation and connection. Cla is related to human relations theory.

The concept of Hierarchy is focused on the internal process model, with internal efficiency and uniformity as its main interests. They have a strong commitment to executing policies and regulations, based on their members' motivation for order, security and rules. The leaders of this type of organization tend to be conservative, cautious and focused on technical problems. Their criteria are control and stability.

The dominance of the Market is consistent with the archetype of the rational goal, tending towards productivity, performance and meeting targets. Oriented towards the external environment to the detriment of internal affairs, the organization focuses mainly on planning, productivity and efficiency. The motivation for adopting this type of culture is based on pursuing and achieving well-defined objectives, including competition and reaching predetermined ends. Leaders tend to be direct, goal-oriented and constantly on the lookout for productivity and structure.

And finally, the idea of Adhocracy is related to the open system model. The term Adhocracy was coined by Henry Mintzberg in 1995, based on an organic, loosely formalized and decentralized corporate structure, in which collaboration is the main characteristic. The structure includes five macro dimensions with different functions and coordination in six different ways. With this perspective, the organization must choose the architecture that best fits the external environment. This model represents a substantial change to the classic model, adapting to today's complex and dynamic environment (MINTZBERG, 1995 *apud* FERREIRA *et al,* 2009). Focused on the external environment, especially flexibility and change, organizations of this model emphasize growth, creativity and adaptation, in an attempt to maximize the individual, risk-taking and anticipating the future. Leaders tend to be entrepreneurial and idealistic, with a willingness to take risks. The criteria for effectiveness include growth, developing new markets and acquiring resources. The figure below represents the Competing Values Framework.

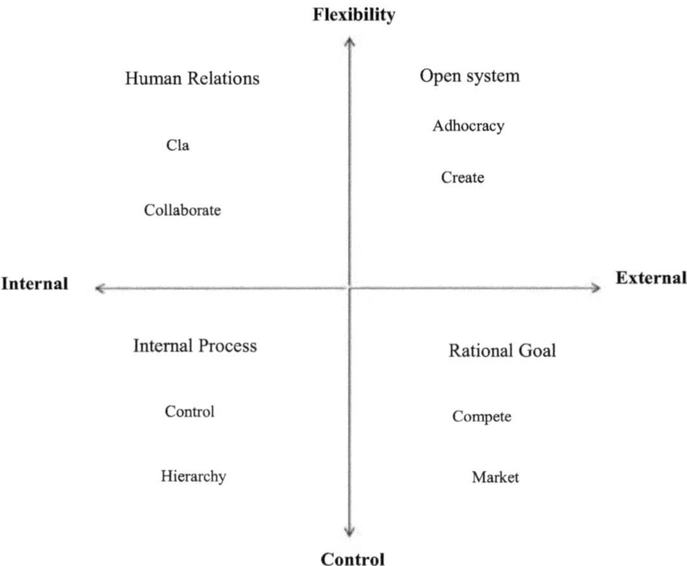

Figure 1: Competing Values Structure
Source: adapted from Quin *et al* (2015)

Figure 1 summarizes the typology of the Competing Values Structure. On the vertical axis are the variables called flexibility and control, while the horizontal axis varies between an internal and external organizational focus. The management models, together with the imperative for managerial action and the dominant culture of this type of organization, are represented in the image. Each model has its opposite. The idea of human relations bringing flexibility and an internal focus is diametrically opposed to the idea of a rational goal anchored by control and an external focus.

The concept of an open system defined by flexibility and an external focus goes in the opposite direction to that of an internal process, defined by control and an internal focus. It is also interesting to note that each concept has a parallel with another. The human relations archetype shares the idea of flexibility with the open system archetype and shares the emphasis on internal focus with the internal process model. The open system ideal and rational goal share an external focus. And the rational goal and internal process archetypes internalize control.

In this section, it was possible to describe the importance of culture and its developments in contemporary organizations. The historical analysis of the concept of culture, relating this concept to the history of management models, has also made it possible to understand the current state of these two variables, thus projecting possible changes in the dominant ideas about management. With this introduction, the next section is dedicated to looking at the main challenges facing organizations when it comes to making a cultural change in their structure.

2.1.2 Cultural change: the main challenges

The culture must be aligned internally and externally for the company to achieve the desired results. The narratives surrounding the context of the organization must be aligned. If the culture is not in line with the characteristics of the people who work there, or the people are not in line with the culture, achieving results can be very difficult. Planned organizational change projects aim to align these points in order to improve people's productivity. A transformational change involves effectively altering the culture to a lesser or greater degree. In the current situation, the model tends to be the one that best suits the demands of the environment in which it is inserted.

In this sense, it is in an organization's interest for change agents to increase their capacity to intervene in the planned process, acting in accordance with the situation of the external and internal environment. To do this, it is first necessary to identify the types of change that can occur in order to develop strategies to deal with each type.

Changes can be classified as first or second order. First-order changes refer to those that affect the system in a more restricted way, representing adjustments to the methods of carrying out tasks. They have a shallower scope in their alterations, relating to the more objective and visible aspects of the company. The second, on the other hand, represent more structural and radical changes, modifying the entire system itself. In this sense, the current currents of work, beliefs, values and the basic assumptions that underpin these practices are analyzed (SIMS, FINEMAN and GABRIEL, 1993 apud SANTOS, 2014).

A distinction can also be made between incremental and strategic changes. The former are those that bring about modifications in specific components of the organization, without, however, it being necessary to change the conception of the strategy being addressed. The introduction of new technologies and changes in personnel management practices are examples of this type of change. In the opposite direction, strategic changes reshape the entire basic framework of the organization, including its *design*, structure, and in more incisive situations, the values that conceived it (NADLER and TUSHMAN, 1990 *apud* SANTOS, 2014).

The authors point out that, within this concept, changes can also be reactive or anticipatory. The reactive form refers to responses to internal pressures, while the anticipatory form corresponds to changes in the macro-environment and an analysis of future scenarios.

Another important distinction in the types of changes is between those carried out spontaneously, planned or directed. The first is characterized by the fact that it does not come from or is not managed by the company's management. In fact, it is generated by changes in the daily lives of employees and guided by people without hierarchical positions. Planned change occurs in a programmed way and is governed by processes and procedures that must be followed by everyone in the organization. Directed management, finally, is characterized by being led by the company's management, through people with positions of authority to supervise and guarantee its implementation (PINTO and LYRA, 2009 *apud* SANTOS, 2014).

For many authors, whatever change they want to implement, whether in the corporate environment or not, tends to be resisted by people or groups. Giddens' (2015) concept that even within a culture some values can be contradictory, giving rise to various codes of behavior, is interesting from this perspective. People who hold power will find it more difficult to adhere to the proposed change in an attempt to maintain the *status quo*. These people can form resistance groups that prevent change. The idea of subculture is therefore formed - groups that reject the dominant values and norms, which can hinder the process. The dominant theory on resistance to organizational change states that this behaviour is an inevitable response, and a major factor in the success or failure of the project. It therefore remains to assess the degree to which this factor will affect the achievement of the objectives set. With this forecast, it is possible to develop measures that minimize the effort so that obstacles can be overcome.

A study carried out by Bortolotti *et al* (2011) sought to analyze the possible behaviors of resistance to organizational change. An adapted questionnaire was used to survey 810 individuals. The majority of respondents answered that they are in favor of change, but a small proportion answered that they may show resistance and indifference. The results corroborate the importance of knowing the attitudes and reactions of people and groups when faced with a proposal for organizational change.

Table 1 shows a summary of possible behaviors in the face of change. Based on the results presented, it is possible to plan preventative measures and alternatives that can mitigate the effects of indifference and resistance to change.

Chart 1: Possible behaviors in the face of change.

	Individual	Collective
Acceptance	- help and warm support; - cooperation; - cooperation under pressure from management; - acceptance; - passive resignation.	- it's a kind of defensive action
Indifference	- indifference; - apathy; - loss of interest in work; - wait; - do whatever is necessary.	- clinging to the old ways of doing things.
Passive resistance	- do only what is ordered - regressive behavior; - not learn; - protests; - work according to the rules by doing only what is told; - rationalize refusing; - apparent acceptance, then back to old ways; - laughter, irony, pleasure at failures; - personal withdrawal (increasing time away from work) - slowing down;	- work to send; - delay diffusion levels.

	- retain information; - feign ignorance; - verbal agreement but not execution (known as white resistance)	
Active resistance	- do as little as possible; - reduce the pace of work; - personal withdrawal; - making "mistakes" - cause damage; - deliberate sabotage; - criticize senior management; - grounds for complaint; - refusal of additional workload; - appeal to fear; - manipulation; - critics using facts selectively, blaming or accusing; - spreading rumors and discussion; - intimidation or threatening, obstructing, undermining; - appeal to fear; - ridicule.	- absenteeism and increased morbidity; - reduced yield in quantity (low productivity) - reduced yield in quality.

Source: Adapted from Judson (1996), Giangreco (2002) and Keneth (1995) *apud* Bortolotti *et al* (2011).

Bortolotti *et al* (2011) also suggest another way in which agents of change deal with resistance. In an attitude of defense, these agents generally do not see resistance as a positive factor, believing that this behavior only arises to oppose the designed process. However, change imposed by force generates a greater amount of resistant behavior in individuals and groups. With this in mind, change agents can opt for an integrative strategy involving the participation of individuals in the design and implementation of the change process, thus encouraging a reduction in the phenomena of resistance and the cooperation of individuals in the process.

On the other hand, Hernandez and Caldas (2001) take a critical and divergent view of resistance behavior. For them, the dominant idea of resistance is constructed according to certain assumptions which indicate that this behaviour is inevitable and natural to human beings, harmful to the organization, exhibited only by employees and in groups. Based on an opposing critique of these assumptions, the authors analyse the process of organizational change based on the individual's perception, from exposure to the stimulus to the adoption of a given behaviour.

The first assumption analyzed is that resistance is inevitable. Hernandez and Caldas (2001), based on studies, showed that it is possible for those involved not only to understand the reasons, but also to cooperate in order to make change projects a success. They concluded that resistance is not a natural behavior and only occurs in specific circumstances. They also realized that agents of change, by trying to avoid or prevent certain behaviors, can hinder the progress of the process, contributing to the occurrence or worsening of resistance.

The belief that resistant behavior is always harmful to the organization is the second assumption of the dominant theory challenged by the authors. For them, these mechanisms can contribute to preserving specific characteristics of the organization. When this occurs in such a way as to preserve important aspects against unnecessary or negative change processes, this phenomenon is healthy and positive. It generates reasonable questions for the change agent, bringing new ways of carrying out the process in an adaptive and innovative way. This assumption is often used as an excuse to justify the failure of change processes that have not achieved the desired success (HERNANDEZ and CALDAS, 2001).

The authors also contradict the assumption that human beings are naturally resistant to movements that alter the *status quo*. Because they object, they tend to use defense mechanisms to react to any threat to the existing balance in order to minimize uncertainty. They argue that human beings crave change and that this need is usually greater than the fear of the unknown.

Another assumption put forward by the dominant theory is that employees at lower hierarchical levels within the organization tend to be more opposed to change. Hernandez and Caldas (2001) state that resistant behavior can be displayed by both employees and leaders. Employees, when they see that change can be beneficial for themselves and their peers, join in and cooperate to make the process a success. The opposite is also true: if they feel that the process is detrimental to them, they don't join in and hinder the success of the project. As far as managers and leaders are concerned, the idea is similar, that resistant behavior can be displayed by those in power (usually at higher hierarchical levels) when they are faced with the loss of their privileges or positions. If the individuals in this group consider that the process will not have a negative impact on themselves, they tend to join in and cooperate with the process of change.

The last assumption refers to the individualization or collectivization of behavior. According to the dominant maxim, resistance is only presented in a mass form. This thinking implies that the members of a company can be classified within a homogeneous group, always acting in an orderly manner, accepting or resisting a certain change. Hernandez and Caldas (2001) start from the counter assumption that within organizations there are no homogeneous groups, and that resistant behaviour can be either an individual or a collective phenomenon. Resistance, therefore, can vary from one individual to another depending on personal and situational factors.

As presented in this section, the main challenges that can manifest themselves in attempts to bring about cultural change within organizations can be identified. It is necessary to understand how these processes can occur, based on the classification of types of change. It is also important to note that the People Management department can act to minimize resistance. The next section highlights some strategies that can be adopted in this regard.

2.1.3 Strategic formulations: Mintzberg's contribution

In order to encourage the process of change, it is necessary to adopt objective strategies that bring the expected results in a sustainable way, within the cost and timeframe previously designed. It's worth first introducing the concept from an organizational perspective.

Mintzberg *et al* (2010) define strategy based on an analysis of what the authors call the "five Ps", claiming that this concept cannot be defined in a simple way, which is why it was necessary to use this division. The first P refers to the plan, i.e. a course of action to guide the future. Thus, it is what the organization intends to do to achieve its objectives.

Pattern is the second P, defined by the authors as the consistency of behavior over a period of time. In this sense, it focuses on the attitudes taken by the organization in the past, seeking to understand how they have defined the present.

The analysis of these first two concepts reveals a very important relationship when it comes to strategy. Organizations draw up plans for the future, trying to extract patterns of behaviour from the past. A distinction is thus made between these two modes, the one that was intended and the one that was actually carried out or, as the authors call it, deliberate strategy. In this sense, there are also actions that were not carried out. There is also a third case which is extremely important for understanding the concept presented here. Strategic actions in which a pattern has been achieved without it having been intended are called emergent. The adjustments that need to be made to the plan so that, over time, it can converge towards a pattern. This model is shown in figure 2.

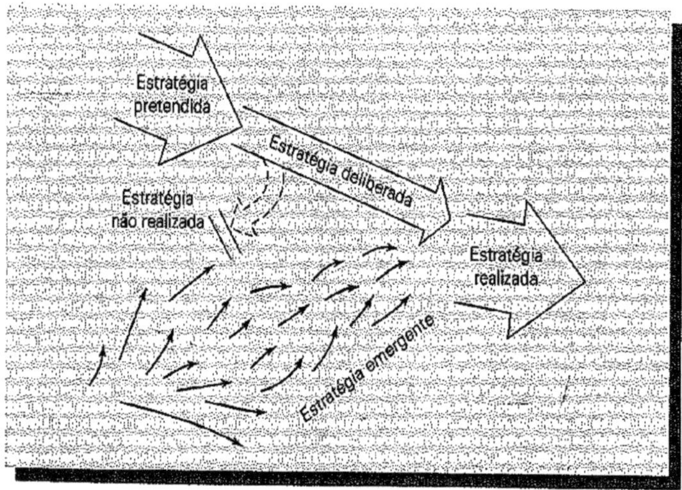

Figure 2: Emergent and deliberate strategy Source: Mintzberg *et al* (2010)

Few strategies are totally deliberate or totally emergent. Strategies must blend these two terms in order to exert control while fostering learning. Therefore, a strategy must form as well as be formulated.

The third P refers to the way in which the organization defines its market positioning, i.e. the location of its products and services in a given market for certain customers. At this point, the strategy is focused on the company's external relationship with its customers, i.e. the best way to approach the end consumer in order to use the products or services.

The P of perspective is aimed at identifying the fundamental way in which the organization carries out its processes. The focus at this point is on the internal analysis of the company's strategy, with the aim of outlining the big vision that must be followed.

The last concept is that of pretext, in which the organization manages to prevail over its competitors. In this case, the company may take a strategic position that is only intended to limit the actions of its competitors.

In this way, the real strategy (as a plan) represents a threat, not the action itself.

With the introduction of the five Ps of strategy, Mintzberg *et al* (2010) classified ten schools that underpin this concept in organizations. Table 2 shows these schools, highlighting the focus that each one places on the process of conceiving and executing strategy.

Table 2: Schools of Strategy

The School of Design:	strategy formulation as a design process
The School of Planning:	strategy formulation as a formal process
The School of Positioning:	strategy formulation as an analytical process
The Entrepreneurial School:	strategy formulation as a visionary process
The Cognitive School:	strategy formulation as a mental process
The School of Learning:	strategy formulation as an emergent process
The School of Power:	strategy formulation as a negotiation process
The Cultural School:	strategy formulation as a collective process
The Environmental School:	strategy formulation as a reactive process
The Configuration School:	strategy formulation as a process of transformation

Source: Mintzberg *et al* (2010)

The first three schools are prescriptive, in the sense that they focus more on the question of how strategies should be formulated than on how they are formed. The others, on the other hand, consider the specific aspects of the formulation process, focusing on describing how they are actually formulated.

Although there is a distinction between the process of how strategies should be formulated and how they are actually formed, models that manage to bring generic concepts can be easier to apply. In this sense, it is worth recalling the contribution of Porter (2014), as discussed below.

2.1.4 Strategic definitions and positioning: Porter's model

Porter (2004) analyzes how an organization can compete more effectively in order to strengthen its position in the external environment. The author states that strategic planning has become widely accepted as an important issue to be addressed in order to chart the company's long-term course. However, there were no rigorously developed tools to respond clearly to this model. He then proposed a conceptual basis for understanding the latent forces of competition in sectors, based on the development of the "five forces" concept. This model demonstrates the differences between sectors and their evolution, encouraging organizations to find a unique position in the market. The author also develops the infrastructure of the concept of competitive advantage, defining it in the models of cost and differentiation, which are directly linked to profitability.

Porter (2004) also states that every organization that competes in a market has a strategy, which can be implicit or explicit. This strategy can be developed through a planning process that is explicitly structured in its formulation, reflecting the proposition that there are significant benefits to using this process. This tends to attest to the fact that the company's policies are planned and led towards a common foundation of goals.

For Porter (2004), development can also be carried out implicitly through the activities of the company's different functional sectors. When it considers only its own means, each sector tends to pursue its own methods of strategic conception and action, driven by the professional guidance and incentives given to each member. In this case, the sum of all these disorganized actions does not usually correspond to the best strategy. Proper strategic management therefore requires truly integrated action, which goes beyond simply putting together a set of initiatives that add up.

The author argues that the five competitive forces are: entry of new competitors, threat of substitution, bargaining power of buyers, bargaining power of suppliers and rivalry between current competitors. Together, they define the intensity of competition between organizations, and the degree of each force depends on the environment itself. The strength of each force will have an impact on the strategy formulation process.

The first force is the degree of difficulty in entering a market, the desire to gain a substantial share or resources. As a result, prices can fall or costs rise, reducing profitability. The threat of entry depends on the barriers to entry that exist in a given market, together with the reaction that established companies will have to the new competitor.

The pressure that companies suffer from competing in a market that, in a broad sense, produces substitute products, is the second force analyzed. Substitutes can reduce returns by setting price ceilings that affect profitability. The products that deserve the most attention are those that have a steadily increasing price-performance ratio in relation to the product or are produced by companies with high profit rates. The higher the price-performance ratio offered by substitutes, the stronger the pressure on market profitability.

Buyers compete with suppliers by forcing prices down, always trying to bargain for better quality or more services, in order to guarantee the profitability of the purchase. Buyer power depends on certain market characteristics (e.g. information asymmetry and competitive situations) and the relative importance of their purchases compared to the total business. This power changes over time and can decrease or increase.

Companies are mutually dependent, i.e. the movements of one organization have an effect on the others. Rivalry between existing competitors in a market is often related to the dispute for position, through the use of tactics such as price, quality, advertising and the like. This is due to the constant need for organizations to try to improve their position in the market.

Suppliers, on the other hand, can exert pressure on buyers by threatening to raise prices or reduce the quality of products and services. Supplier power can greatly reduce the profitability of the industries of buyers who are unable to pass on costs to the customer. Therefore, the conditions that make suppliers powerful tend to reflect those that make buyers powerful. These conditions are also subject to change over time.

Considering the analysis of the five competitive forces, Porter (2004) states that strategies are offensive or defensive actions aimed at creating a position to confront these forces, thus increasing the organization's profitability. There are several ways to achieve this goal, and each way is a unique solution for a given organization, reflecting the internal and external conditions particular to it. However, the author states that, by adopting a broader analysis, it is possible to find three generic strategies that can create a long-term profitable position to outperform competitors.

Generic strategies are methods of outperforming competitors in the market. They can be used alone or in combination, and can also translate the generic concept into specific actions for each particular situation. The three approaches outlined by the author are total cost leadership, differentiation and focus.

The total cost approach consists of achieving leadership through a set of policies geared towards this goal, which requires building facilities on an efficient scale, constant reductions in costs and overheads, among other related actions. This tends to give the company a solid position in relation to the five forces, with above-average profitability. Low cost in relation to competitors is the central theme of this model, without ignoring other variables such as quality and price.

The model for differentiating the product or service offered is based on the intention to create something that is considered unique in the market. In the broadest sense, organizations differentiate themselves along various dimensions that can provide a defensible position against the five competitive forces. Differentiation provides insulation from rivals due to consumer loyalty to the originality of the product. It can also increase margins by excluding the need for low cost. It is important to stress that this strategy does not allow costs to be ignored, but they are not the primary target.

The third strategy is to focus on a specific buyer group, product segment or geographic market, and can take a variety of approaches. The focus aims to meet the specific target that has been determined, focusing the strategy on meeting this objective. The premise here is that the organization is able to meet its target more effectively and efficiently than competitors who take a broader position. The company can meet its particular target by having lower costs or product differentiation, thus assimilating itself to another generic model. This model can support a potential increase in profitability, which sustains a position against competitive forces.

Moving from strategy formulation to execution is a component that raises empirical questions for organizations. Mellon and Carter (2015) present another methodology they call execution strategy, which consists of five steps. The first step consists of mobilizing the "village", here understood as the group of executives who are in the middle hierarchy of the organization. The authors believe that the main bottlenecks to execution lie with this group. They must therefore be the first to be convinced and mobilized if the process is to succeed. In order to involve this "village", it is necessary for each of its members to see themselves as part of this community. They also need to be given a sense of ownership of the process.

The second step adopted is to gather the partners, who are defined as a small group of senior executives who work alongside the *Chief Executive Officer* (CEO) to carry out the strategy. This village is led by this select group, which is why they should be the second group to denote a sense of ownership of the process. The role of the ancients in this case is to transform the members of the village into confident followers who can drive the execution of the strategy.

Empowering the emotional is the third step of this methodology. Adopting a different way of thinking is how you create purpose and give meaning to your work. A new strategy also involves a process of change, and this requires a new perspective for people. In order for people to acquire the sense of ownership to make a change, it is necessary to adopt a more emotional than rational content, thus enhancing the emotional nature of the process. Ideally, you should focus on changing people's set of beliefs, so that this becomes evident in their actions, which makes a change effective. To carry out the strategy, it is therefore necessary to mobilize people through persuasion and engagement.

Once the previous three steps have been carried out, it is necessary to stimulate people through three variables: communication, a sense of ownership and continuity. Those involved must understand the purpose of the change through an effective communication process. A sense of ownership is acquired by providing encouraging experiences and giving them the space to carry out the strategy. And through deliberate continuity, what has been proposed will be improved and innovated.

The last step in an effective execution strategy is to create "resilience". The authors define this term based on its components: resilience, adaptability and perseverance. Resilience refers to the ability of both the organization and individuals to recover quickly from any adversity and stay on course with the strategy. Adaptability consists of the high level of adaptation required to be able to recover and learn to live in a new format. And finally, perseverance is defined as the necessary energy that keeps people focused on achieving their goals.

Mellon and Carter (2015) state that by adopting this methodology it is possible to involve people rationally and emotionally, making the process of executing the strategy a less arduous journey.

Having taken up some of the main foundations of strategic management, as discussed here, the next section highlights how the processes of strategic formulation and execution impact on people management.

2.1.5 Impact of strategic formulations on people management

The process of formulating and executing strategy has a direct impact on the performance of People Management (PM). Considering the current context in which knowledge is the most valuable organizational resource, people have become an extremely important factor for the success of any organization. The more qualified, trained and prepared workers are, the greater the competitive advantage for the business. People, therefore, provide the competitive edge for the organization. In this sense, people management must be an essential component in the formulation and implementation of any organizational strategy. The strategies adopted become essential to the success of the organization. The incorporation of the PM strategy with the company's macro strategy determines the actions and attitudes in people management, directly impacting on the success of the enterprise.

For management to be even more strategic, it needs to act as a business partner, providing support for all other areas. Its strategy must be based on the assumption that this activity should not just be an objective-functional component within the organization. It is necessary to create a sense of belonging for people:

"HRM practices are seen as vehicles for the construction of meanings and "stories" about people - who they are - and about the organization - its distinctiveness and coherence. "HRM is not seen as an objective-functional system, but as a meaning-making tool that organizational members use to develop and reproduce meanings about who they are and what their firm represents." (ALVESSON & KARREMAN,2007. Page 2 - free translation).

In order to become more than a functional objective within organizations, People Management must include strategies that seek to integrate people in the face of the fragmented and departmental vision of companies. Internal consultancy is the process by which organizations seek to integrate themselves into the Strategic People Management model, denoting greater agility in their practices. The aim of this practice is to broaden the scope of action in the constant search for knowledge and innovation. In this context:

[...] organizations have been consolidating the role of People Management and expanding the role of HR professionals as Internal Consultants, capable of boosting changes, people's energy and knowledge, improving organizational structure, speed and quality (GIRARDI et al, 2009).

Thus, internal consultancy has taken on an important role as a management support activity, acting as a systemic vision. Internal consultancy aims to provide decentralized information to the organization, as well as offering better service to internal clients (LIMONGI-FRANÇA, 2006). The consultant must act as an agent of organizational development, with the ability to develop behaviours, attitudes and processes that are in line with the planned change strategy.

Internal consultancy is the result of the evolution of People Management itself, from a legalistic bureaucratic area to the current stage of strategic alignment with the demands of the organization, and acts as a tool for organizational change. The redefinition of management involves the decentralization of its activities and practices, allowing it to emerge as a strategic agent. This agent adds significant value to organizations by getting to know companies' problems and contributing creatively to the organization's productivity and efficiency. The process aims to value people with a focus on knowledge, shared development and competitiveness (GIRARDI *et al*, 2009).

People Management strategies also cover the levels of competencies that its professionals must possess so that the area can contribute to the organization's development. Ulrich *et al* (2012) developed the concept of HR from the inside out, which is based on the premise that the area is the business itself, transforming strategy into results for the organization as a whole. Business strategies should be understood as the way in which the area observes, interprets and translates the external conditions and expectations of all *stakeholders*. Professionals must know how to organize and deal with these conditions in order to place the organization in a strategic position in the present and in the future.

The authors believe that in order to operate in this new model, professionals need to move within six paradoxes. They draw on their research into the competencies of professionals, carried out over twenty-five years by the *Human Resource Competency Study (HRCS)*. The six competencies or paradoxes are the professional as: Trusted activist; Strategic positioner; Capacity builder; Champion of change; Innovator and integrator of human resources and Proponent of technology.

The first paradox refers to the integrity of the professional in the field. As a trustworthy activist, they must deliver what they promise and their results serve as the basis for personal trust, transforming it into professional credibility. They possess effective interpersonal skills, managing to deal harmoniously with their *stakeholders*. They translate this skill and professional credibility into results for the business.

As a strategic positioner, the high-performance professional must understand the global business context - such as social, economic, political and other related issues. They have knowledge of their company's structure and that of other competitors, understanding the competitive dynamics of the market in which they operate. They are therefore able to express this understanding in business implications, using the knowledge to develop visions for the company's future.

The *effective* professional must also create, audit and manage an organization that is efficient in defining and creating its organizational skills. The capability builder must help area managers to create meaning so that the capabilities of the company's members reflect its deepest values. These capabilities go beyond the behavior or performance of any one member, they are something deeper that emanates from the individual's values.

Developing an organization's capacity for change means that the PM professional needs to translate this component into effective change processes and structures. They must also have the ability to create change situations based on the reality of the market and the business that overcome the resistance of the main *stakeholders*. The integration of change processes is intended to create a sustainable competitive advantage for the business, given the instability of the corporate environment.

The knowledge of innovating and integrating practices around a few critical business issues is the fifth paradox defined by the authors. Professionals must ensure that business results are prioritized around appropriate organizational capabilities and well-structured processes and practices. The challenge is to make the whole of GP more efficient than the sum of its parts. Innovation and integration of practices, processes and structures lead the area to have a more significant impact on business results.

In the role of technology proponents, PM professionals are involved in two categories. Firstly, they use technology to help people (*stakeholders*) connect, both inside and outside the organization. Secondly, they act as information managers within organizations, identifying those that are strategic and most critical.

In this section, it was possible to observe the process of formulating and executing strategy, bringing these concepts to the People Management area. The next section looks at the history of the area and the contributions it has made to organizational management.

2.2 People Management and its contributions

The history of People Management (PM) goes hand in hand with the evolution of business organizations based on the concepts of Scientific Management. For a long time, this function was an objective-functional area within the institutionalized hierarchy. Initially, it was responsible for work accounting and bureaucratic records, and was known as the Personnel Department. Later, the area took on other activities and was renamed the human resources department. This concept incorporated activities such as training, development, remuneration and other similar activities (Wood *et al*, 2012). At that time, people were seen only as a factor of production, similar to machines.

In recent decades, the concepts surrounding the area have undergone changes, corroborating a functional evolution of the area within the business hierarchy. The emergence of knowledge has meant that people have become a competitive advantage for organizations. This moment allowed for conceptual and structural changes, which in short were positive for the evolution of the area. By taking on a narrative of alignment with strategy, it has been constantly decentralized since then. It has become common for companies to outsource activities that are extremely operational. The redefinition of management involves decentralizing its activities and practices, allowing this strategic agent to emerge.

The current format of GP is still under construction, allowing strategic trends to be added to the area and presenting challenges for its future. The Fourth Industrial Revolution will directly affect people's relationship with their own work, and consequently will demand a different approach to the one adopted today.

2.2.1 Anthropological justification

Since the dawn of time, *homo sapiens* have possessed a difference that has been fundamental to their survival and evolution as a society compared to other species: they are the only ones capable of creating fictions and believing in them, thanks to their unique language. The language of the Sapiens is quite versatile, being able to unite innumerable sounds and signs to communicate an infinite number of messages to a growing range of people (who share the same mode of communication); the Sapiens are thus able to consume, store and communicate an extraordinary amount of information about the world around them. (HARARI, 2015)

The fiction created not only made it possible to imagine things in an individualized way, but also made it possible to use this unique language collectively, engendering socialization and the development of cooperation models that allowed this evolution to take place. The characteristic that allowed this language to be unique is the ability to communicate narratives about things that don't actually exist. "All large-scale human cooperation [...] is based on shared myths that only exist in people's collective imagination" (HARARI, 2015, p. 33).

The narrative created collectively from the myths and symbols shared in people's collective imagination gave *sapiens* the ability to cooperate around the same goal and in large numbers. Persistent belief in imagined and shared myths influences reality. An imagined reality is something that everyone believes in and, as long as this shared belief persists, the imagined reality exerts an influence on the world (HARARI, 2015).

Based on this anthropological concept, it is possible to conclude that narratives are a mechanism for mobilizing people that has proved effective in the evolution of contemporary society. By this definition, the assumption adopted here is that well-developed narratives allow people to cooperate around the same purpose. Isn't this, in the first instance, the basic structure of a business organization?

However, the narratives that have guided the world in past centuries have their origins in Cartesian systems, such as Taylor's time and motion studies, in which it is claimed that there is a scientific way of managing people that is similar to managing machinery:

"Remarkable savings in time and the consequent increase in output can be obtained by eliminating unnecessary movements and replacing slow and inefficient movements with fast ones in all trades." (TAYLOR, 1990, p. 33). These narratives were based on "absolute truths" that supported the systems, and they worked because people believed them. The fictional entities of society, such as the State and the Church, are the fruit of this narrative.

Although human cooperation is based on myths, this same cooperation can be altered if the myths change, starting with a different narrative. In contrast to the traditional narrative, other narratives have changed and altered its meaning for people. The Cartesian narrative can no longer mobilize people's emotions and actions in society as it used to. These new narratives dissolve the belief in an "absolute truth", in blind trust in reason. This causes a dissolution of the idea on which the entire previous system was based. The fictional entities continue to act in the same way as before, but people don't agree with the previous narratives in an entrenched way. Social organizations can no longer maintain their form for long. They break down and dissolve faster than the time it takes to shape them (BAUMAN, 2007). The family, the church and the state, for example, do not have the same configuration as before.

In organizations, the disintegration of these narratives has been no different. People continue to work, but the production system can no longer engage them in the same way as before because the narrative that sustained it has weakened:

Traditional management theories have proved limited in keeping up with the turbulence that characterizes contemporary society. [...] Management models built from this perspective aim to create the conditions for pre-determined results to be achieved, believing that there are always cause and effect relationships that can be mapped and controlled (FERREIRA; CARDOSO; CORRÊA; FRANÇA, 2009, p. 164).

The complexity of today's world, marked by uncertainties, does not allow for analysis as was previously done in the belief in an absolute truth, and it is necessary to adopt a less deterministic perspective. Thus, instead of the old reductionist, Cartesian perception, it is necessary to achieve a new, post-Cartesian vision, which is still in its infancy.

Despite taking into account the turbulence of the environment, traditional theories can only contemplate the idea of incremental change. The current environment, however, presents a number of disruptive situations that demand a more incisive attitude towards change from the organization. Therefore, traditional management models are failing to meet the demands imposed by the environment and must evolve towards a non-linear assessment of situations, using less simplistic models of cause and effect predictability:

In this new perspective, science is seen as a kind of multidimensional map, with boundaries that are not too rigid between the various disciplines and with bridges that promote a constant exchange between them (MORIN apud FERREIRA *et al*, 2009, p. 170).

The question that arises from this observation is how to manage these people in the current situation. Companies in the so-called disruptive economy (in which various sectors are breaking with old models to meet consumer demands) are examples of companies that currently manage to unite sapiens within their narratives. The answer is that organizations must adapt to the changes the world is undergoing in order to remain competitive.

2.2.2 Historical evolution of the People Management area

The function of People Management in organizations began with the intention of accounting for employees' clock-in and clock-out times, so that we could control the time they spent at work and pay them according to the time they spent working for the organization. Scientific Management, advocated by Taylor and Fayol, among others, was the basis for the creation of this control function, a pioneer in people management. In this phase, people were seen as an additional tool, no different from any other available tool, for the organization to achieve its objectives. It was the production manager himself who managed his subordinates, and the function of what was then known as the Personnel Department was simply to account for costs and pay employees. This moment is defined by Tose (1997) as the accounting phase.

In Brazil, from 1930 onwards, a process of legalization of work began, defined by the Consolidation of Labor Laws (CLT). At this time, the new function of People Management began to be exercised in a different way, since the new work model required compliance with labor laws. This led to the training of the head of personnel, who also had to deal with the new legal issues imposed on the workplace. This phase is referred to by Tose (1997) as the legal phase. Power within the organization, which had previously been exercised only by the head of production, was now also exercised by the head of personnel.

Fischer (2002) brings another approach to the two phases mentioned above. The author condenses the accounting phase and the legal phase, mentioned by Tose (1997), into a single phase which he calls the Personnel Department (PD), an area focused "primarily on procedural and bureaucratic transactions" (FISCHER, 2002, p. 19). The Personnel Department identified employees as a factor of production, as much as a machine, which had to be managed like any other cost of production. Scientific Management was compatible with the structure and function of the PD of accounting control of costs and the search for workers who are efficient in scientifically ordered activities.

The writings of the Human Relations School, which began in 1920, brought about a paradigm shift in management, and consequently in the role that the human resources area plays within the organization. The Hawthorne studies carried out by Elton Mayo and his team also revealed the importance of psychological and social aspects at work and how they can influence productivity, differentiating themselves from the hypothesis of economic man put forward by Scientific Management (LACOMBE; HEILBORN, 2008, p. 311). The concept put forward by this school is that it is necessary to eliminate or minimize existing conflicts between labour and capital in order to reduce costs and increase productivity, taking into account the informal structure of the organization. This movement began to change the role of the head of personnel, substantially changing his focus. The concern became managing the individual's needs within the organization (MARRAS, 2011).

The head of personnel now has to manage production costs relating to people, ensure compliance with labor laws and manage the relationship between employees and employers. At this point, the body came to be called Human Resources and ceased to have an extremely operational function and came to be seen in a more tactical way, and to be considered in the organizational hierarchy as a management, according to Marras (2011). It can therefore be concluded that this context allowed for a more orderly and organized management of the human resources area. The worker began to be managed as a technician, with the vision of a specialist.

According to Tose (1997), this phase is called technicist. In Brazil, it began in the 1950s, mainly due to the entry of multinationals, a move facilitated by Juscelino Kubitschek's economic policies. These companies applied advanced techniques for managing people, putting pressure on competitors in the domestic market to incorporate certain techniques. This pressure led to the need for personnel managers to use more robust control and techniques for selection, training, performance evaluation and job and salary analysis.

In this historical context, it is necessary to put People Management (PM) practices in Brazil into context. Organizational and PM theories originated abroad and arrived in Brazil through a process of colonization and neo-colonization. Colonization took place through the introduction of basic management practices such as recruitment and selection, training and development. "[...] The import and implementation of human resources models and practices played an important role in the professionalization of companies" (WOOD *et al*, 2011, p. 234). The second phase, called neo-colonization, was characterized by better alignment with business objectives, "through the adoption of decentralized structures and the creation of jobs for internal consultants" (WOOD *et al,* 2011, p. 236).

According to Fischer (2002), this phase is known as Human Behavior Management, where the main concern of People Management was to help the production line manager exercise his leadership over the workers in the best possible way. The role was to train the manager, improve performance evaluation processes and align the managerial profile with the profile desired by the company. "Motivation and leadership became the key concepts of the humanist model" (FISCHER, 2002, p. 21). This phase can be summed up in three main axes: economic effectiveness, technical effectiveness and behavioral effectiveness.

From 1965 to 1985, the administrative or unionist phase developed. According to Tose (1997), at the beginning of this period, the Brazilian state intervened incisively in the relationship between employee and employer, acting on both sides of the relationship. While it intervened in social security legislation, wage policy and union organization, preventing workers' movements, the state also influenced the training and qualification of human resources professionals, bound by legislation that prevented them from acting. In the 1970s, trade unions increased their mobilization of workers, leading to the resurrection of the trade union movement known as "new trade unionism" (TOSE, 1997). During this phase, human resources were focused on the organization's relationship with the workers' unions. Negotiations between employers and workers' unions became extremely important for organizations, requiring a professional capable of dealing with the paradox between company and worker, avoiding strikes and production stoppages (MARRAS, 2011). In this context, the Human Resources function has become even more important, acting in conjunction with company management and representing it in negotiations with workers.

In the course of the evolution of administrative theory, the systemic and contingency approach has influenced the structural and functional organization of companies.

Consequently, the Human Resources area has also been impacted. This approach sees the organization as a whole made up of mutually integrated parts, inserted in an environment with which it constantly interacts. The organization is therefore seen as an open system, which influences and is influenced by the environment in which it operates (LACOMBE; HEILBORN, 2008). As an evolution of systemic analysis, contingency theory addresses the idea that there is no single correct way of structuring an organization; each organization has its own specific structure depending on the environment in which it operates. Based on this concept, the structures of organizations began to adopt specific models for their environment, adopting a more holistic approach to the performance of their structures (LACOMBE; HEILBORN, 2008). In short, the human resources area has undergone profound changes in its structure with this new approach. Only the notion of the School of Human Relations and Behaviorism that people need sufficient working conditions to achieve objectives did not become effective in terms of results. The external environment influenced the company's actions, requiring strategic HR action.

This new understanding, allied to the process of evolution of the People Management area, as already highlighted, allowed the area itself to take a more strategic stance. According to Tose (1997), the function of PM at this stage was to seek the best possible action based on internal policies and environmental factors. The area began to be introduced into the macro strategy of organizations, in which there was a concern for the long-term performance of management practices. During this phase, it became common for companies to outsource activities that are extremely operational, such as health care, restaurants and payroll. This process freed up human resources professionals to think strategically in the long term, focusing on people management and the integration of the company's areas. It is possible to observe a delegation and a return of power to line managers in a process of partnership between the areas, where people policy is centralized but implementation is decentralized.

Tose (1997) and Fischer (2002) call this phase strategic. For Tose (1997), this is the current phase of Human Resources, which is still in the process of being built. Fischer (2002), however, adds a fourth and current phase where the model is structured by competencies and competitive advantage. In this author's view, Porter's theories of competitiveness and Hamer and Champy's Reengineering led to a new model of company organization, culminating in a concept of Human Resources focused on competitive advantage through the competence of people. People began to be seen as a strategic resource for the organization in order to achieve a differentiated position in the market.

The delimitation by phases was structured as a methodology for analyzing the performance of the people management area. There are two analyses that can be made from this distinction. The first is that these phases are not found in a pure state in organizations, and there are remnants of previous phases today. The second is that not all companies are in the last phase of evolution, whether it's the strategic phase, defined by Tose (1997), or the competitive advantage phase, named by Fischer (2002). In light of these considerations, it is possible to identify and position the area of management that will be analyzed, based on the definitions of each moment presented, and to outline objectives to achieve a strategic character and an effective role in the organization's results.

3 METHODOLOGY

This chapter highlights the main methodological aspects followed in the research whose results are presented here.

3.1 Guidance

The research has a mixed approach. Both quantitative and qualitative concepts are used. However, the qualitative characteristics were predominant, due to the difficulty in quantitatively measuring the actual process of cultural change.

The quantitative part is evidenced by the application of the *Organizational Culture Assessment Instrument* (OCAI) questionnaire developed by Quinn *et al* (2015). The data obtained from this instrument was analyzed using basic statistical formulas. Below is a breakdown of the form and how the data obtained was analyzed.

The conclusion and qualitative analysis were made from the researcher's point of view, as he was involved in the problem over a period of time, evaluating the actions that were planned and the consequences of these events.

3.2 Universe and sample

The universe studied were the managers and members of the administrative areas of a multinational company in the automobile industry located in the city of Juiz de Fora - MG. Table 3 shows the general information about the application. The applications totaled 177 respondents divided into nine areas. The applications were carried out by the management team of the organization in question, together with the researcher, who was a member of the team at the company studied.

The focus of this study was the project implemented in the administrative areas. It is important to note that at the time the company had around 800 direct employees and around 1,200 indirect employees.

Table 3: OCAI General Framework

GENERAL CHART		
AREA	ANSWERS	% TOTAL
GROSS	10	6%
PAINTING	10	6%

FINAL	8	5%
ACCOUNTING	17	10%
IT	6	3%
LOGISTICS	60	34%
OLI	28	16%
PLANNING	8	5%
QUALITY	30	17%
TOTAL	177	100%

Source: survey data

3. 3 Data collection

The project began with the application of a questionnaire called the *Organizational Culture Assessment Instrument* (OCAI) developed by Quinn *et al* (2015). The questionnaire was developed to analyze organizational culture based on the competing value structures discussed in the theoretical framework. The structures used in the study were the Cultures of Cla, Hierarchy, Adhocracy and Market, whose fundamental characteristics are detailed in the theoretical framework. The form used, shown in Table 4, consisted of twenty-four questions divided into six blocks, each block containing four statements.

The application consisted of instructing the respondent to divide by one hundred percentage points those statements that were most similar to their organization, giving them the highest score. Each answer was related to one of the four elements of the chain of competing values, which were then tabulated.

Each block had its own related theme: the first block referred to the organization's dominant characteristics; the second referred to the organization's leadership; the third referred to people management; the fourth referred to organizational culture; the fifth condensed the organization's strategic emphasis and finally the sixth referred to the success criteria adopted.

Table 4: OCAI form

	AFFIRMATIVES	POINTS	
O	The organization is results-oriented. People are competitive and performance-oriented		
9	The organization is very personal, like the extension of the family. People share different aspects of their lives		1 - Dominant
Cfl	The organization is a well-structured and formal place. Formal procedures govern the way people act		characteristics
	The organization is dynamic and entrepreneurial. People are willing to take risks		
CM	The role of the organization's leadership is to guide, facilitate and develop its members		
O	Leadership is about coordinating, organizing and making the organization more efficient		2 - Organizational
The	Leadership is focused on entrepreneurship, innovation and generally takes a lot of risks		Leadership

	Statement		Dimension
Cfl	The main focus of the organization's leadership is results		
BLOCK 3	The management style is characterized by security, compliance and predictability		3 - People management
	The management style is characterized by competitiveness, high demand and meeting targets		
	The management style is characterized by taking risks, innovating and giving freedom to create unique things		
	The management style is characterized by teamwork, consensus and participation.		
o The co	What holds the organization together is loyalty and trust. Commitment to the organization is high.		4- "Glue" that holds the organization together
	What holds the organization together is innovation and development. There is the motivation to always be at the top		
	What holds the organization together is an emphasis on results and achieving goals.		
	What holds the organization together are formal rules and policies.		
1Л o The co	The organization emphasizes acquiring new resources and creating new challenges, as well as seizing new opportunities.		5 - Strategic Emphasis
	The organization emphasizes competitive actions and individual achievements. The aim is to be dominant in the market.		
	The organization emphasizes permanence and stability. Efficiency, control and standardized operations are important.		
	The organization emphasizes human development. Trust, openness and participation persist.		
BLOCK	The organization defines success on the basis of its products, which are unique or newer.		6 - Success criteria
	The organization defines success based on its position in the market. Competitiveness is the key dimension.		
	The organization defines success based on human development, teamwork and commitment.		
	The organization defines success based on its efficiency. Production costs are important.		

Source: Adapted from Quinn *et al*, 2015

To prevent the answers from being biased, there was no sequence for each item in the competing values structure. The statements for each model were placed randomly to prevent respondents from repeating the same answer for all the items.

4   THE COMPANY IN FOCUS AND ITS CHANGE PROJECT

The company that is the subject of this study is a multinational automobile manufacturer with four branches in Brazil, three of which are located in the state of Sao Paulo and one in the state of Minas Gerais. In Brazil, it has been producing trucks, vans, buses and cars for 60 years. It is one of the largest in Brazil in its field, producing vehicles for the domestic and foreign markets. The study in question was carried out at the Minas Gerais branch. The plant in question was inaugurated in 1999 and began manufacturing cars.

At the end of 2016, a new process of change began, and this was the focus of the study. At this time, the plant was undergoing a shift in production, with strategic alignment with the headquarters in Sao Paulo. The factory started producing all the cab models needed to finish production at the headquarters.

The constant changes taking place on the world economic scene were also a backdrop for the People Management (PM) department to initiate the project. The emergence of a technological revolution, which brings with it the almost unrestricted automation of industries, is also a factor that alters the relationship between organizations and society.

The next section highlights the main characteristics of the change project implemented by the People Management (PM) department of the unit studied.

4.1 The process of change in 2016/2017

The cultural change project in question was drawn up by the unit's People Management team and is in line with the group's macro strategy for the coming years. The scope of the project is designed to take around two years, with six months per phase. This study analyzed the development of the first and second phases of the project in the company's administrative areas, focusing on the performance of People Management and its impact on the other areas.

To guide the project, we used Robert E. Quinn's (2006) competing values methodology, already mentioned in the chapter that presented the theoretical framework. In every business organization, there are four basic values that are mutually related and are influential in the company's organizational culture. On the one hand, there are the internal values, called Cla and Hierarchy, according to the terms presented in the previous chapter. On the other, there are the external characteristics, called Innovation and Market.

The project has been divided into four phases, to put these concepts into practice and change the culture of the people who work in the organization. The first is routine management. In this phase, the manager of each area must go over with his team the routines that are currently carried out and question them so that people can identify those activities that add value and those that don't to the general purpose of the area. The aim is to eliminate activities of low importance, relieving people of these unproductive activities and preparing the team for the next phase.

The second is process management. Here, the manager and his team are prepared to map the processes carried out by the area, taking into account the optimization of the routine in the previous stage. A process is understood here as a set of routines carried out for a specific purpose. The focus in this phase is that only the activities that effectively generate value for the company remain.

The third phase is project management. Here, the team must be motivated to work with a more strategic mindset, viewing the area's processes holistically. The processes must integrate projects that increase effectiveness and efficiency, in line with the area's purpose.

The fourth phase is called *Coworking*. Here, the team is encouraged to work together by sharing space and work tools, encouraging the exchange of ideas and collaboration between team members.

As a way of managing the project, management tools were applied that enabled the development of innovative products that could withstand change. The project management model used is based on Scrum, in which it is possible to check at regular intervals that the project is going in the right direction and that the product that will result from the project is really what people want. The aim of the methodology is to improve the productivity of the team taking part in the project.

The methodology had to be adapted for People Management projects, with a focus on team autonomy and productivity. The planning consisted of adapting this model, taking into account the activities carried out by the PM and those that required the attitude of the manager. A presentation was developed with standard graphs for daily visualization of the project's progress in each area of the company.

With this practical design combined with the group's global narratives, the aim is that, by the end of the project, all areas of the company will be acting in a more integrated and cohesive manner, generating greater value for the company.

4.2 Analysis of the change process

The planned process of change effectively began in November 2016, with the People Management (GP) area applying the project to the other administrative areas. The eleven administrative areas were included, accounting for a total of one hundred and seventy-seven people. As part of this work, the first phase of the project was analyzed for all the administrative areas.

The strategy adopted was to divide the program into PM functions and define the functions for the leader (manager) to do with the team. In this sense, once the PM has taken action and delivered his products to the areas, the manager has a reaction to encourage the team to make the planned change. Each phase of the project is structured into twelve steps. Each is related to the actions of the manager and the PM to support the culture change. From step one to five, this is called the Deployment moment, in which the team is motivated to question the current work routine. From step six to nine, there is the so-called Development moment, marked by the restructuring of the work agenda, criticizing activities and eliminating those that do not add value to the area. From the tenth to the twelfth step, this is called the Stabilization of Change moment, when the team must leave with an optimized agenda so that it can begin the second phase of the project (analyzing the area's processes).

The first GP action in the areas was to introduce the manager to the workings and strategy of the whole change process. After the manager's acceptance, the invitation was made again, with the presentation of the operation and strategy, to the other people in the area in order to generate a sense of ownership of the project. With the acceptance of all the people involved, the project began with the application of the questionnaire called *Organizational Culture Assessment Instrument* (OCAI) developed by Quinn *et al* (2015).

This section presents the analysis of the change process in each administrative area. Firstly, it is necessary to identify the company's general strategy with regard to this planned change process. According to studies by Quinn (2015), by applying the OCAI questionnaire (Figure 3), it was possible to detect that vehicle manufacturers are more focused on the values of Cla and Hierarchy, i.e. their internal processes, than on market needs and innovations. It can therefore be assumed that, in order to adapt to these changes, the company is slightly biasing its organizational culture towards external characteristics, innovation and the market. Since this change is the company's strategy, the point is not to deny the internal characteristics, which are actually the company's strengths and which have brought it to its current position over the last century. It's just to slightly tweak the company's values in order to adapt to the current way the market and society behave, as shown in figure 3 below.

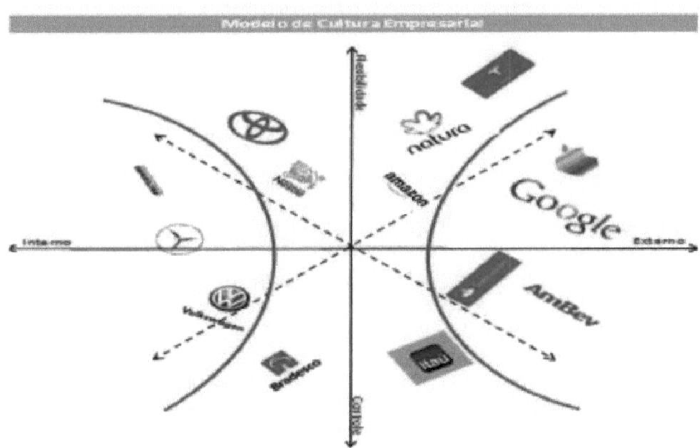

Figure 3 : Corporate Culture Models - OCAI

Source: Adapted from Quinn (2015)

Figure three shows the general information after applying the questionnaire. Figure 4 shows a general illustration of the organization after applying the first form.

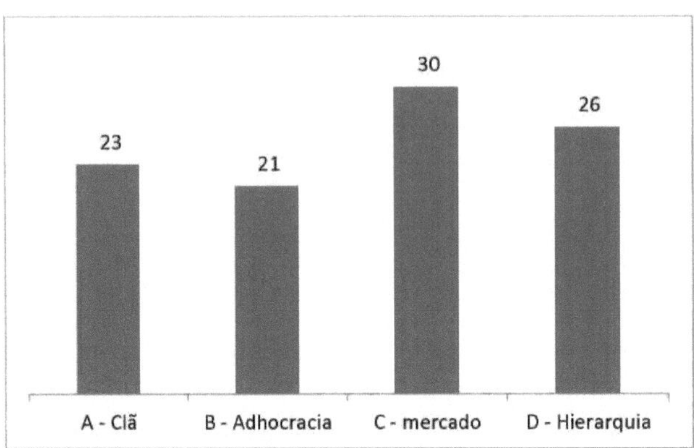

Figure 4: OCAI General Graph

The analysis of the data shows that the organization's managerial employees have a greater tendency towards Market values, related to productivity, performance and the achievement of targets. They also have a strong tendency towards Hierarchical values, such as internal processes and uniformity. It can be seen that the data obtained from the application of the form differs somewhat from what would be expected from the study by Quinn et al (2015), shown in figure 3. According to these authors, car manufacturing organizations focus on values relating to the internal characteristics of the organization, tending towards the clausal and hierarchical models.

In the project we analyzed, the managers of each area are very important in conducting the activities as a whole. The manager's behavior and commitment are fundamental to ensuring that the group members are not reluctant to follow the program's objectives. For this reason, the OCAI questionnaire was analyzed for the managers of each area in order to identify the characteristics of each one in terms of the model they identify for their area. This analysis is important in order to allow GP to take a personalized approach to each one, increasing the assertiveness of the proposed actions. Figure 4 shows the results of this questionnaire.

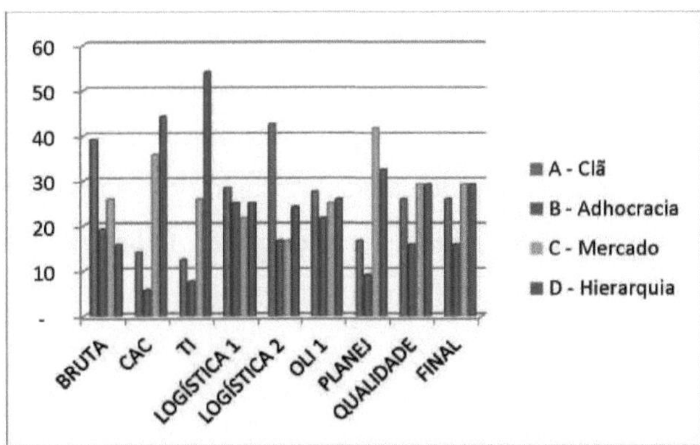

Figure 5: OCAI Managers graph

The data obtained by applying the questionnaire to the members of each area is analyzed below, in an attempt to bring out the context faced by the People Management (PM) area when applying the project.

4.3.1 Painting

The Painting Department carries out activities such as anti-corrosion treatment, surface painting and wax protection. There are ten administrative staff in this area, all of whom responded to the form. The figure below shows the results obtained.

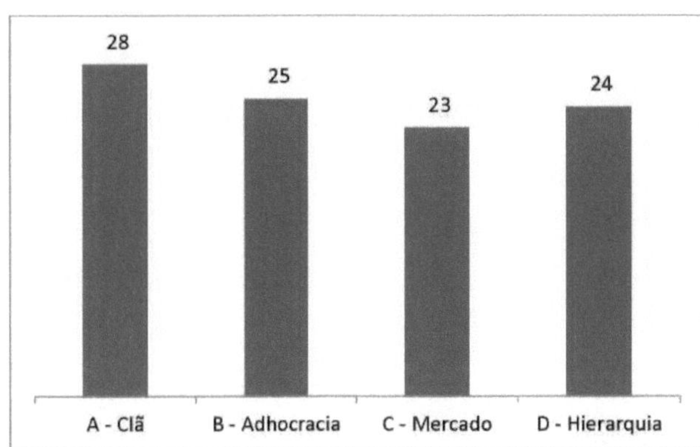

Figure 6: OCAI Painting result

The area's results differ somewhat from those obtained by the organization as a whole. This team's main concern is the maintenance of the group itself, based on the values and objectives shared by the people.

The painting department was very important to the development and acceptance of the project in the unit, as its team was the first to start the project and became a kind of multiplier of the strategy and concepts it addressed. Through oral and visual storytelling strategies, the relevance of the project for the future of the unit was communicated, so that people (including the GP herself) became engaged in the activities.

4.3.2 Rough assembly

The Gross Assembly area is responsible for producing the gross bodywork: adding the lower and side structure and closing the sides. Adjustments and funneling of moving parts, dimensional control and welding are component activities of this block. The administrative part of this area is made up of ten people who answered the questionnaire.

The data collected allows us to infer that the area has a vision focused on the external environment, consistent with the organization's overall results. Internal values have a correlated weight for this group, as evidenced by the scores for the hierarchy and cla models. A weak point in this group is the external view of innovation. Below are the results obtained:

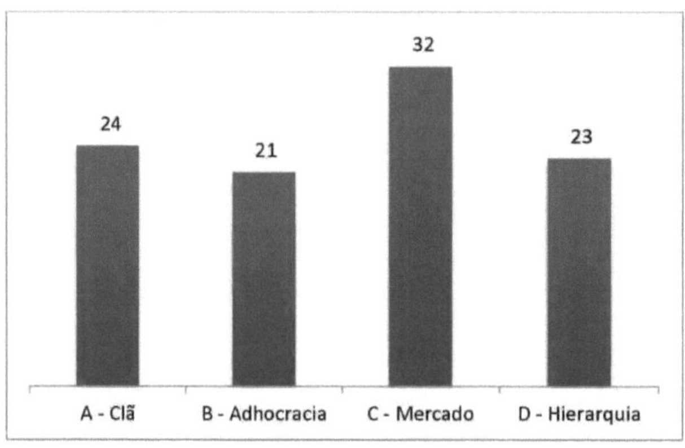

Figure 7: OCAI Gross Assembly result

4.3.3 Final assembly

Completing the production process is Final Assembly, where all the vehicle's internal finishing is added, as well as mechanical assembly and mechanical and final overhauls. The scope of these three production blocks includes continuous improvement processes, problem-solving and process monitoring. The area is currently responsible for finalizing the assembly of one type of heavy-duty truck that is produced at the plant.

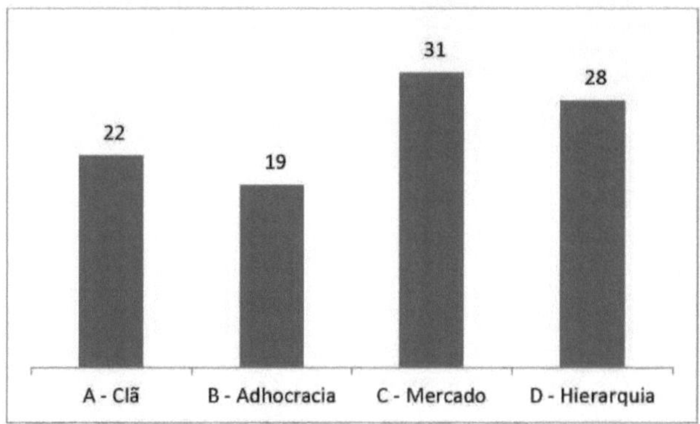

Figure 8: OCAI Result Final Assembly

Figure 8 shows that the area has a market-oriented vision, which is explained by its direct contact with the manufacture of the final product for the customer. At the same time, however, it has a very hierarchical outlook due to the processes that delimit the entire sphere of work. Because of this, people are much less inclined to innovate.

4.3.4 Logistics

The Logistics area is responsible for the entire process of purchasing and delivering materials directly linked to production, including customs clearance of parts from the headquarters in Germany. It has a large number of people in the administrative sector (60 people) compared to the others.

As it is an area with a large number of people and critical processes directly linked to production, the GP had greater difficulty in programming the project. It can be seen from the results of the OCAI questionnaire that the members of the department have a tendency towards the market model. Much of this is explained by the direct contact with suppliers and the final product. However, it is an area that does not have a high degree of innovation and is unable to translate this contact with the market into new management models for the company. Figure 8 shows the results of the form applied.

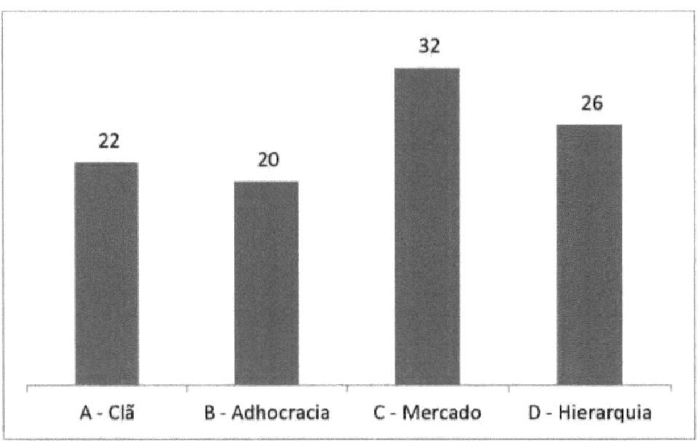

Figure 9: OCAI Logistics result

4.3.5 OLI

The area known as OLI is responsible for all of the plant's technical infrastructure, both in the unproductive and productive parts. It is responsible, for example, for everything from improving the toilets to the technical cleaning of the production area. It has a large number of contracts within its scope, managing a large number of third parties responsible for carrying out these activities.

Analyzing the result obtained by the OCAI (figure 9), it is possible to see that the area has a tendency towards the Market model, explained by the fact that it manages a large number of companies. Like the logistics area, it is unable to reverse this contact into innovations in its processes and management model. It also has a tendency towards hierarchy, requiring the active participation of the manager in activities.

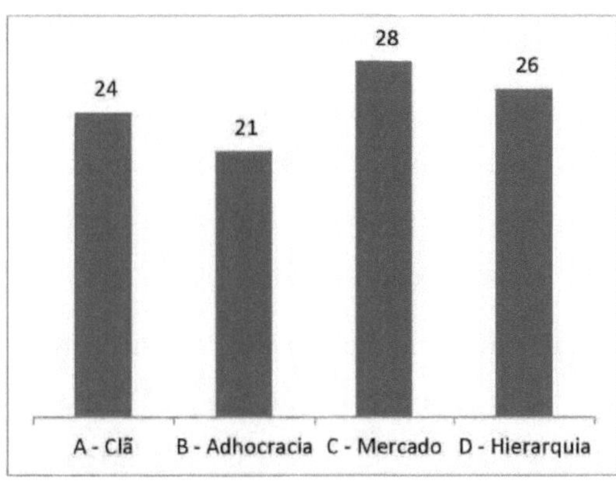

Figure 10: OCAI OLI result

4.3.6 Quality

Quality is the area responsible for maintaining product aspects as determined by the head office, in addition to international technical quality standards. Below is the result obtained from the form.

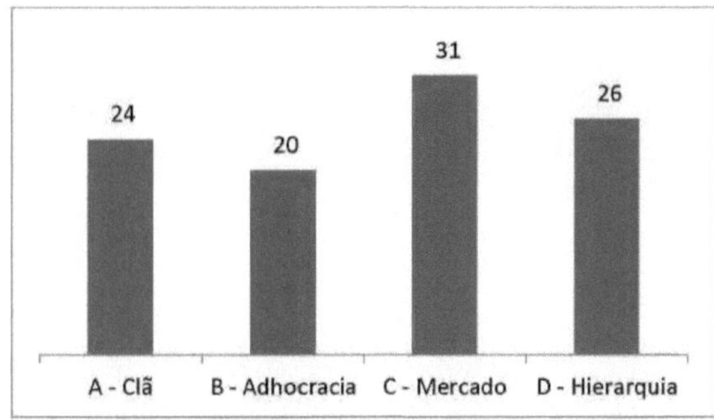

Figura 11: OCAI Result Quality

The results of the OCAI show that the members are inclined towards the market model, with a tendency towards hierarchical management. However, they do not identify with innovating their processes, since they are responsible for replicating international technical quality standards. The aim of the project is to bring this oxygenation to the area's processes, understanding that it is of the utmost importance for the future development of the factory's products.

4.3.7 Planning

The Planning sector is responsible for all innovation projects and the implementation of new models on the production line. They deal directly with the production process, defining the quantity to be produced and how it will be produced. It's a small area (eight members), but it has an important strategic importance for the unit.

Taking into account the small number of members and the fact that they are directly linked to the head office, the PM thought it best to unite the Planning and IT areas in the development of the project so that they could work together. Also taken into account were the characteristics of the managers shown in Figure 7, in which it is possible to see their tendencies in relation to management models.

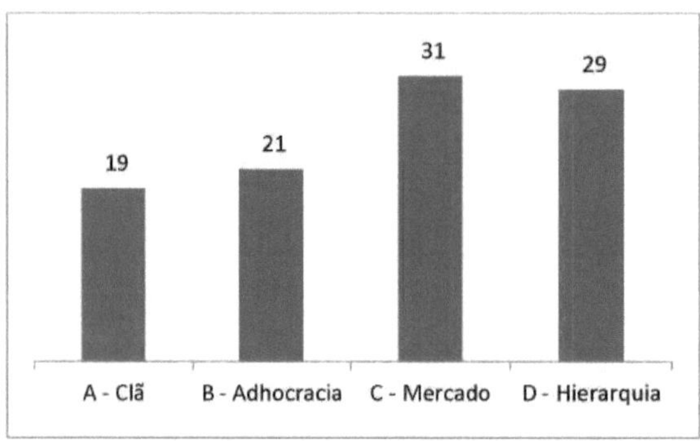

Figura 12: Result OCAI Planning

Figure 12 shows the results of the OCAI applied to the planning area. Like their manager, the members have a greater tendency towards market management, but are also very attached to hierarchy.

4.3.8 Information Technology (IT)

The Information Technology area is responsible for storing, obtaining, transmitting and manipulating data, as well as developing and analyzing the factory's *software* and *hardware*. As highlighted in the analysis of the Planning sector, the two areas were managed simultaneously by the PM area, as a strategic way of moving the project forward.

Figure 13 shows that the people in the department have a very market-oriented outlook, with little regard for the cla and adhocracy models. These characteristics allow us to infer that although the department has a tendency towards external analysis, it is unable to transfer this knowledge to internal processes in an innovative way.

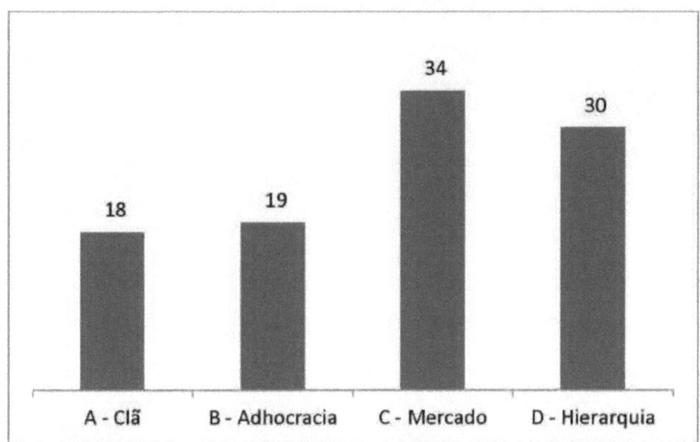

Figure 13: OCAI IT result

Analyzing Figures 7 and 12, it is possible to establish a counterpoint between what the members of the department and the manager think of as the ideal model. While the area has a movement towards the market model, the manager is characterized by a tendency towards hierarchy. This contradiction had a major impact on the development of the project in the IT area, since the members were not free to participate actively in the activities.

4.3.9 Accounting

The Accounting department is responsible for the financial management of the factory, from the entry and exit of materials and finished products. It is responsible for a very critical process for the unit, which is the annual inventory of parts and finished products. His management is directly linked to the head office.

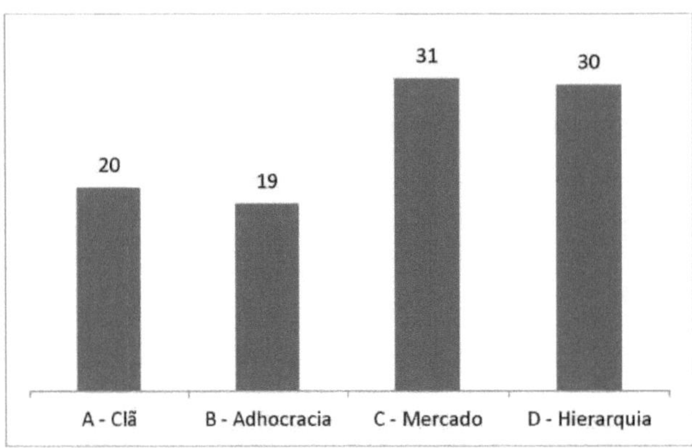

Figure 14: OCAI Accounting result

The members of the area, due to their hierarchical nature (figure 14), supported by the profile of the manager, were not enthusiastic about the program.

4.4 Final data analysis

The data shown made it possible to analyze the cultural change proposed by People Management, and its impact on each administrative area of the company in which the project was implemented. The first phase analyzed was routine management. In this phase, the manager is responsible for improving the routines developed by his team, so that people can identify the activities that add value and those that do not. The aim is to eliminate activities of low importance, relieving people of these unproductive activities and preparing the team for the next phase.

The action of the People Management (PM) department at this time was of the utmost importance for the development of the program. Project management based on the application of management tools based on the Scrum model was essential for supporting change in other sectors. The daily monitoring and benchmarking of the PM's activities was effective for the progress of the project. Figure 15 shows an example of how this management was carried out for each area.

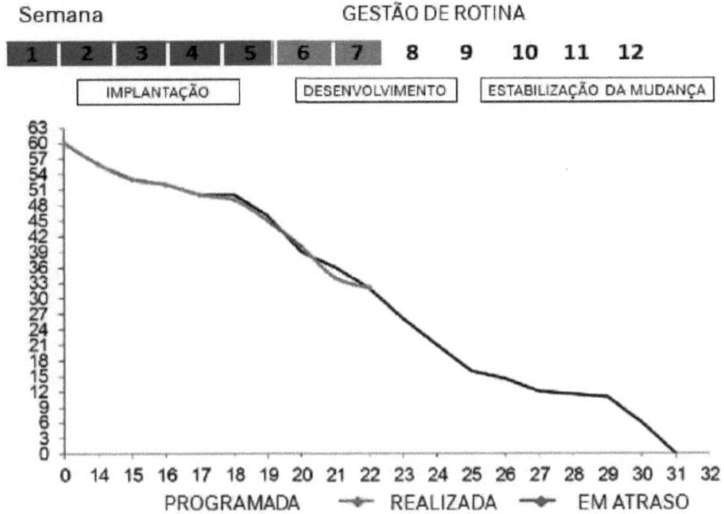

Figure 15: Project management by GP

All the areas participating in the project have completed this first stage, achieving the goal of gaining the time needed to develop the activities that add value to the unit.

The second phase is process management. At this point, the manager and his team are prepared to map out the sector's processes, based on improving the routine from the previous stage. Processes are defined as a set of routines carried out for a specific purpose. The aim is to keep only those activities that effectively generate value for the company and that are all linked to a greater objective, i.e. the purpose of the area. The start of this project is characterized by the definition of the purpose by all team members, which will guide the definition of the processes that should be maintained and the activities that should add to these processes.

The physical changes made to the *layout of* the administrative sector were fundamental to the development of a change in people's mentality. This process aims to focus on grouping people together and not dividing them up by area. The aim of this strategy is to prepare for the project phase and the subsequent completion of the *coworking* model.

An important factor in this process of programmed change is the importance that the training sub-area has been given in this regard. The development of the activities in the

61

other areas demanded behavioral and technical preparation from the People Management staff so that the concepts could be applied. In this sense, employees needed prior training to be able to replicate the expected concept. All GP members became training instructors, in order to help the areas go through the change process with the least behavioral resistance and the greatest possible technical knowledge. This concept is strategic for the project and for the PM area within the unit, as it would bring the areas closer together and make the sector even more strategic and participative in the unit's main projects.

The continuity of the project as a whole, still going through two critical stages for effective cultural change, is a challenge for the People Management department. Despite this, the proposed structure is well conceptualized and the management model implemented can support this demand, since the project has been gaining ground internally in the unit and in the company's other subsidiaries. The model for replicating this project is being developed by GP and could be replicated in the company's other units.

5 FINAL CONSIDERATIONS

As highlighted, the research whose results are presented here sought answers to the central question of analyzing the performance of People Management (PM) in the face of a planned organizational culture change project and how this performance favored this process. By analyzing the quantitative and qualitative data presented, it was also possible to meet the specific objectives of the study, which helped to achieve the general objective.

We found that the cultural change project, which began at the end of 2016, is still underway at the unit. The time frame used to analyze this work made it possible to analyze the evolution of the project up to the halfway point, the first and second phases of the project in the administrative areas of the company, with a focus on the performance of People Management and its consequences in the other areas.

The project made it possible to unite the two major lines of research in the study of organizational culture, as elucidated in the theoretical framework. Firstly, it treated culture as a variable (external and internal), which can therefore be altered through a programmed process of cultural change, as is being carried out. The second sees culture as the foundation of the organization itself, something that is intrinsically linked to its history. This perception has allowed the strategy of adapting the organizational culture to external characteristics to be carried out, with a focus on innovation and the market. It is also worth pointing out that the strategy is not to deny the characteristics that have allowed the organization to remain in the market over the last century. The aim is to change the organization's values in order to adapt to the way the market and society behave today.

The activities of the People Management (PM) area are being strongly impacted as the project develops. The objective of changing the old view of Human Resources to the current and proposed model for the future of People Management (PM) is taking place in a substantial way. This strategic point of the program for the area itself has already been elucidated in the theoretical framework, which is consistent with the need for HR to be more than just an objective-functional component within the organization. Its function should be to create a sense of belonging for people, forming narratives that can create an effective link between the organization and its workers.

The internal separation between the processes that are effectively linked to the cultural change project and those that are intended to support the organization in other ways has been important for the progress of the joint activities. To this end, the activities of these processes are constantly reviewed, so that only those that add effective value to GP's business and the factory as a whole remain.

Two major problems still perpetuate project development in the PM area. The first relates to the quantitative measurement of PM activities in relation to the program, i.e. what financial and economic return the project is bringing to the organization. The second refers to the issue of convincing people to join the project directly, in the sense of taking ownership of the project and continuing it without the direct involvement of management.

The first problem has been much discussed since the beginning of the project, but without a clear definition of which quantitative indicators are best to show the results obtained. Without detracting from the qualitative aspect, the quantitative evaluation reflects the effective economic dimension of the practices adopted. Traditional indicators persisted in evaluating qualitatively, or when they evaluated quantitatively, they only reached the surface of economic measurement. This problem still persists, and the intention is to hire an external consultancy firm to help with it.

The second issue interferes greatly with the activities of the area in general, since the volume of activities increases greatly as the project is consolidated and all the administrative areas are integrated. The feeling of ownership of the project that the areas should have does not occur in all groups, requiring corrective actions and demands from the PM to ensure that the project goes ahead as planned. GP has been studying a set of actions aimed at the internal public, especially those who are most adherent to the proposed project. The aim is for these people to become multipliers of the proposed idea and to transmit this image to the rest of the factory. This practice is of the utmost importance for the continuity of the project, allowing GP to move forward according to the strategy developed.

For future studies, it is suggested that this new People Management model be analyzed in order to bring new concepts and objective results to organizations, as it is a fundamental factor for the development of knowledge in the area itself. The concept of training that has been addressed in this new model also deserves attention.

6 REFERENCES

AFFONSO, N. S. Automobiles and Sustainability. *Instituto de Pesquisa Econòmica Aplicada - Ipea,* Brasilia, v. 53, year 6 aug/2009. Available at

<http://www.ipea.gov.br/desafios/index.php?option=com_content&view=article&id=1049:catid=28 &Itemid=23> Accessed on 01/07/2017

ALVESSON, Mats; KÀRREMAN, Dan. Unraveling HRM: Identity, Ceremony, and Control in a Management Consulting Firm. *Organization Science,* Vol. 18, No. 4, July-August 2007, pp. 711723. Free translation

BAUMAN, Zygmunt. *Culture in the modern liquid world.* Rio de Janeiro: Zahar, 2013.

. *liquid Times.* Rio de Janeiro: Jorge Zahar, 2007.

BORTOLOTTI, Silvana Ligia Vincenzi; JUNIOR, Afonso Farias de Sousa; ANDRADE, Dalton Francisco de Andrade. *Resistance to Organizational Change*: Evaluation of Attitudes and Reactions in a Group of Individuals. SYMPOSIUM OF EXCELLENCE IN MANAGEMENT AND TECHNOLOGY - SEGET, 8, 2011. Resende RJ, 2011.

CARRIERI,Alexandre de Pàdua. Culture in the context of organizational studies: A brief state of the art. *Revista Eletrônica de Administraçà da UFLA.* Lavras, n.1, Vol. 4, 2002

CARRIERI, Alexandre de Pàdua; SILVA, Alfredo Rodrigues Leite; SOUZA, Mariana Mayumi Pereira de; PIMENTEL, Thiago Duarte. Contributions of discourse analysis to organizational studies. *Revista Economia & Gestão da PUC Minas.* Belo Horizonte, n° 12, vol 6, 2006.

FERREIRA, Victor Claudio Paradela, CARDOSO, Antônio Semeraro Rito, CORREA, Carlos José and FRANÇA, Célio Francisco. *Management Models.* 3 ed. Rio de Janeiro: Editora da FGV, 2009.

FISCHER, André Luiz. A conceptual and historical review of people management models. In: FLEURY, Maria Tereza Leme (Org). *People in the organization.* São Paulo: Gente. 2002. p. 11-34.

FLEURY, Maria Tereza Leme. Stories, myths, heroes: organizational culture and work relationships. *Revista de* Administração *de empresas,* São Paulo, Oct./Dec.1987.

FRANÇA, Ana Cristina Limongi. *Human Resources Practices - HRP*: Concepts, Tools and Procedures. São Paulo: Atlas, 2009.

GIRARDI, Dante Marciano;LAPOLLI, Édis Mafra Lapolli; TOSTA, Kelly Cristina Benetti Tonani. *Internal Human Resources Consultancy as a Practice that Catalyzes Knowledge Management.* Revista de Ciências da Administracdo, v. 11, n. 25, p. 121-150, Sep/Dec 2009.

GIDDENS, Anthony. *Sociology.* Porto Alegre: Artmed, 2005.

GOOBI, Gabriel Zamboni. *Culture as a factor of financial success in organizations, based on the Competing Values Framework*. 2012. 73 p. Dissertation (Degree in Production Engineering) - University of São Paulo School of Engineering, São Carlos, São Carlos-SP.

HARARI, Yuval Noah. *Sapiens - a brief history of humanity*. Porto Alegre, RS: L&PM, 2015.

HERNANDEZ, José Mauro da Costa; CALDAS, Miguel P. Resistência à mudança: uma revisão crítica. *RAE - Revista de Administração de Empresas*. Sao Paulo, n.2, Vol. 41, pp. 31-45, Apr./Jun. 2001

LACOMBE, José Masset; HEILBORN, Gilberto Luiz José. *Administration*: principles and trends. 2ª edition. Sao Paulo: Saraiva, 2008.

MARRAS, Jean Pierre. History of Human Resources. In: Marras, Jean Pierre. *Human resources management*: from operational to strategic. Sao Paulo: Saraiva, 2011. p. 513.

MINTZBERG, Henry; AHLSTRAND, Bruce; LAMPEL, Joseph. *Strategy safari: a route through the jungle of strategic planning*. Porto Alegre, Bookman, 2010.

PERASO, V. What the 4th industrial revolution is - and how it should affect our lives. *BBC Brasil*. Sao Paulo, Oct. 2016. Available at <http://www.bbc.com/portuguese/geral-37658309#orb-footer> Accessed on: July 1, 2017.

PORTER, Michael E. *Competitive strategy: techniques for analyzing industries and competition*. Rio de Janeiro, Elsevier, 2004.

QUINN, Robert; FAERMAN, Sue; THOMPSON, Michael; MCGRATH, Michael; BRIGHT, David. *Managerial competencies: the competing values approach to management*. Rio de Janeiro: Campus, 2015.

SANTANA, D. L. de; MENDES, G. A.; MARIANO, A. M.. Study of Hofstede's cultural dimensions: comparative analysis between Brazil, the United States and Mexico. *C@LEA - Revista Cadernos de Aulas do LEA*, Ilhéus, n. 3, p. 1 - 13, nov. 2014.

SANTOS, Marcel de Souza e Silva. *Organizational Change Management*: A theoretical review. 2014. 106 p. Dissertation (Master's in Business Management) - Getúlio Vargas School of Business and Public Administration in Rio de Janeiro.

SCHEIN, Edgar. *Organizational culture and leadership*. Sao Paulo: Editora Atlas SA, 2009.

SCHWAB, Klaus. *The Fourth Industrial Revolution*. 1st edition. Sao Paulo: Edipro, 2016.

SHIBA, Soji; GRAHAM, Alam; WALDEN, David. *TQM: four revolutions in quality management*. Porto Alegre : Bookman, 1997

TAYLOR, Frederick Winslow. *Principles of scientific management*. 8th edition. Sao Paulo: Atlas, 1990

TOSE, Marilia de Gonzaga Lima e Silva. *The evolution of human resources management in Brazil*. 1997. 127 p. Dissertation (Master's in Administration). School of Economics, Administration, Accounting and Actuarial Sciences, Pontifical Catholic University of Sao Paulo, Sao Paulo, 1997.

ULRICH, Dave; YOUNGER, Jon; BROCKBANK, Wayne; ULRICH, Mike. *HR from the inside out: six competencies for the future of human resources*. Porto Alegre: Bookman, 2013.

WOOD JR, Thomas. TONELLI, Maria José. COKE, BILL. Colonization and neocolonization of human resource management in brazil (1950-2010). *Revista de Administração de Empresas*. Sao Paulo, n.3, Vol. 51, pp. 232-243, May/June 2011.

WOOD JR, Thomas. TONELLI, Maria José. COKE, BILL. Where is people management going? *Getulio Vargas Executive*. Sao Paulo, n.2, Vol 11, pp. 20-24, Jul/Dec. 2012.

I want morebooks!

Buy your books fast and straightforward online - at one of world's fastest growing online book stores! Environmentally sound due to Print-on-Demand technologies.

Buy your books online at
www.morebooks.shop

Kaufen Sie Ihre Bücher schnell und unkompliziert online – auf einer der am schnellsten wachsenden Buchhandelsplattformen weltweit! Dank Print-On-Demand umwelt- und ressourcenschonend produzi ert.

Bücher schneller online kaufen
www.morebooks.shop

info@omniscriptum.com
www.omniscriptum.com

Printed by Books on Demand GmbH, Norderstedt / Germany